Managerial Communication for Professional Development

Managerial Communication for Professional Development

Reginald L. Bell
Jeanette S. Martin

BEP BUSINESS EXPERT PRESS

Managerial Communication for Professional Development
Copyright © Business Expert Press, LLC, 2019.

First published in 2019 by
Business Expert Press, LLC
222 East 46th Street, New York, NY 10017
www.businessexpertpress.com

ISBN-13: 978-1-94999-113-0 (paperback)
ISBN-13: 978-1-94999-114-7 (e-book)

Business Expert Press Corporate Communication Collection

Collection ISSN: 2156-8162 (print)
Collection ISSN: 2156-8170 (electronic)

Cover and interior design by S4Carlisle Publishing Services Private Ltd., Chennai, India

First edition: 2019

10 9 8 7 6 5 4 3 2 1

Printed in the United States of America.

Dedication

To our spouses, immediate family members, and students:
Our heartfelt thanks to our families for allowing unfettered time on
weekends to work on the book and for your patient support. We are grateful
to our students for their input on ideas and topics that were necessary
inclusions for this second edition.

—Reginald and Jeanette

Abstract

Managerial Communication for Professional Development offers a unique functions approach to managerial skills. It explores what the communication managers actually do in business across the planning, organizing, leading, and controlling functions when professional skills are needed the most. The Windows into Practical Reality adds contemporary information pertinent to key concepts in the chapters. Focusing on topics such as public image, impression management, reprimanding employees' unproductive behaviors at work, effective presentations skills, employment communication best practices, and claims and argument missteps managers make during crisis. The contents of this book will help managers and future managers understand the professional development skills essential to management communication functions.

Keywords

argument; audit; career; change; coaching; commitment; crisis management; delegation; employment; figures of speech; financial reporting; hierarchies; image; impression management; leadership; laws; legislation; negotiating; presentation; professional development; reprimand; stakeholders; strategic planning/career development; teams; technical core; training/workplace learning; trust; value chain

Contents

Preface

Purpose

Managers engage stakeholders at all levels of communication (intra-personal, interpersonal, group, organizational, and intercultural) which requires professional development skills. Expounding on theories of rhetoric and claims as arguments that require proof, the authors relate them to the theories of management—such as persuasion and influence, syllogistic logic, and warrants, qualifiers, and reservation arguments that might not be favorable to the persuader. These are the personal skills of speaking, writing, listening, and doing that are invaluable to management.

Contents

The book includes six chapters emphasizing the essentials of managerial communications for top, middle, and frontline managers engaged in the four functional areas of planning, organizing, leading, and controlling.

The book is especially useful for managers and mid-career working adults enrolled in MBA programs, as there are many examples to which they can relate. The materials will also serve as guideposts for professors doing research and teaching in the managerial communications field. Professors with little or no industry experience will find the chapters' contents replete with workplace examples. Professionals and future managers will find the contents of the book engaging and refreshing due to the real-world approach. Currently, there is a gap between academic research and business practice linking managerial problems to communications solutions. This book sheds light on particular techniques of management communication as they are used by people engaged in managing others at each level of the organization and across the various functional areas.

Reginald L. Bell, PhD

Jeanette S. Martin, EdD

Acknowledgments

Thanks to Our Editor

We appreciate the honest and accurate feedback received from Debbie DuFrene, our editor, who helped us tremendously with this second edition of our book. The features, figures, tables, charts, and graphs were all made much better because of Debbie's meaningful comments; her untiring efforts were essential in shaping this book. We appreciate her surgical pen and feel that her insistence on points of view, technical details, and painstaking adherence to specificity has made this book a useful tool in preparing professionals to resolve management problems that require well-developed communication skills. She ensured that balance was adhered to with the presentation of representative views on both sides of controversial issues, especially in the Windows into Practical Reality features in each chapter. We also appreciate the efforts of others who reviewed the book's chapters and materials.

CHAPTER 1

Effective Presentation Skills

Objectives

After reading this chapter, you will be able to:

1. describe the parts of a presentation;
2. explain the elements of presentation purpose, preparation, and delivery;
3. discuss how to use emotional intelligence to make presentations more effective;
4. identify patterns of speech that can make language more inspiring and persuasive;
5. design effective charts, graphs, and tables.

Introduction

While giving an oral presentation is the number one fear that many people have, mastering the art of the presentation is essential to becoming a successful leader. Doing so will allow you to be a leader who possesses the ability to connect positively with your employees or audience. If you know what is important, and you get that message across, you are on your way to being an effective leader. To be a good leader, you must understand your strengths and weaknesses, have a vision and passion that others can see, be willing to take risks, be a good communicator, and produce results. It is not easy to persuade, inform, and entertain your audience in order to reach their emotions or to move the audience to action. Developing the ability to influence people will take preparation and perseverance. Remember that a presentation is only effective if the audience changes their beliefs or actions, obtains more information, or merely enjoys being entertained.

Managers need to know what they want to accomplish when they give a presentation. In this chapter, we will discuss the fundamentals of presentation: (1) purpose, preparation, and delivery; (2) speech dangers and filled pauses (FP); (3) using emotional intelligence; (4) using figures of speech; and (5) proper use of charts, graphs, and tables.

Purpose, Preparation, and Delivery

The three essential elements of an effective presentation are purpose, preparation, and delivery. Each aspect is critical to achieving effective results. As you begin thinking about a planned presentation, you must first understand the purpose of your presentation. What do you want the audience to know? Then select the appropriate type of media for that purpose.

Purpose

Your purpose can be to persuade, inform, or entertain your audience. Each of these purposes has a corresponding objective. When you *persuade,* you convince someone to believe what you are telling him or her—you are changing his or her mind. When you *inform,* you are giving the individual information or facts that they need. When you *entertain*, you are making someone feel good, such as telling a joke or finding something of common interest to talk about.

Busy customers, clients, and company personnel will give up moments of their precious time to listen to your presentations. Delivering an effective presentation is imperative. There is an old cliché to which many business people can still relate: "If you don't have time to do it right the first time, where will you find the time to do it right a second time!" The measure of any good presentation is the accomplishment of the speaker's purpose.

Let us consider the possible objectives of each presentation type:

- Persuasive presentations can be designed with an objective to
  - cause a change in belief
  - cause a change in immediate actions

- Informative presentations can be designed with
  - a narrative objective
  - a descriptive objective
  - an explanatory objective
- Entertainment presentations have an objective to offer gratification, achieved when your audience experiences a sense of satisfaction.

Your audience will need to feel a sense of satisfaction, regardless of the purpose of the presentation. When the audience is unsatisfied, achieving your purpose and objective is jeopardized. Table 1.1 shows examples of a presenter's purposes and objectives for various speaking occasions.

In climbing the managerial ladder, most people eventually reach a level of responsibility where they are required to give a presentation from time to time. Motivating lethargic and even demoralized employees with vivid and vital language is often times required. Presenting a business plan before a review board to secure financing for a project is part of many managers' tasks. In both cases, the manager must use language that is applicable to the audience.

Table 1.1 Purposes, objectives, and occasions for differing oral presentations

Presentation purposes	Presentation objectives	Presentation occasions
To Persuade	To cause a change in belief by persuasion To cause a change in action by persuasion	Legal arguments Political arguments Debates Group conferences Sales/promotional talks Proposals
To Inform	To inform by describing To inform by explaining To inform by narrating	Classroom lecture Oral reports (eulogy, dedication, commemoration, acceptance, introduction, acknowledgment, etc.) Factual reports Manufacturing reports Annual reports
To Entertain	To cause gratification overlaps all three purposes of presentation	After-dinner presentations Lectures on popular themes Travel talks Monologs Award presentations

One example of an effective persuasive presentation might be an appeal for the approval of the budgeted amount for pay increases. Giving the presentation to a budget committee for a large, nonprofit organization just before an annual budget review is very common. The desired result of the presentation would be to get the board approval of an increase in the line-item amount for employee salaries. The presenting manager's purpose would be to be persuasive, the objective would be targeting a change in the board members' actions (the board actually approving the raises), and the occasion is selling or promoting the pay raise idea.

An example of an effective informative presentation is for a middle manager seeking to inform all 25 frontline supervisors about a crucial procedural change for an assembly-line operation. The stated purpose is informative. The objective in this case would be explanatory, showing the benefits of a change in the way of doing things. The occasion would be a conference room setting or small classroom. This personal approach would be more effective than sending an e-mail message.

If the speaker's purpose is merely to entertain, the rules governing that purpose are somewhat different. An example would be a 2-minute after-dinner presentation congratulating a colleague on a promotion or an extraordinary accomplishment. While the primary objective of an entertaining presentation is audience gratification, the element of gratification is present in all three types of presentations. Do not leave your audience unsatisfied, regardless of your purpose.

Sometimes the news delivered in a presentation is dreadful, such as in Franklin D. Roosevelt's (FDR's) war address. But the speech did not come without gratification, which was in the president's planned response to Japan's aggression. Later in this chapter, we will look more closely at FDR's war presentation.

Preparation

Preparation requires organization because too much of disorganized information can be overwhelming for both the presenter and audience.

All presentations have three main elements. The *introductions* function is to tell them what you will tell them (TTWYWTT). An example would be: "Today we are going to discuss the development of the new production line for Crispy Treats." The *body's* function is to tell them (TT). An example would include covering the main points known about the production line for Crispy Treats. Finally, the *conclusion's* function is to TT what you just told them: TTWYJTT. The example here would include a summary by the presenter of the major points, and then the floor would be open for a discussion. The acronyms for these three major elements are helpful when you organize your presentation materials.

Good organization is essential for an effective presentation. Getting organized includes brainstorming, researching your topic, and developing an outline. Before you research the topic, organize your ideas into a rough draft of main points (MP). Develop the first-draft outline by talking aloud and writing down what you already know about the topic. Thoroughly research the topic to refine your knowledge on that subject. Researching articles and books, performing interviews, or finding information on the Internet can increase your knowledge on your targeted topic. Developing your outline helps you organize your ideas into a rough draft of MP. Subordinate points (SP) extend the logical unfolding of the MP, as shown in Figure 1.1.

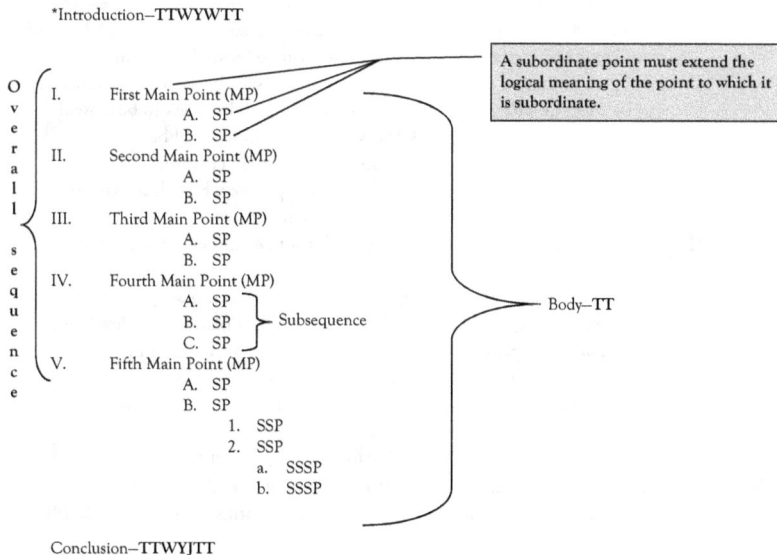

Figure 1.1 The main parts of a presentation

Roman numerals precede MP; capital letters of the English alphabet precede SP; Arabic numerals precede sub-subordinate points (SSP); and lowercase letters of the English alphabet precede sub-sub-subordinate points (SSSP). In the rare case, a SSSP would need to be extended use lower case Roman numbers to precede SSSSPs. The outline in Figure 1.2 illustrates an MP on financing a small business startup. Note that each MP should have at least two sublevels of the logical extension reflected by its SPs.

After you have determined the purpose of your presentation and the organization of content, you need to determine how best to deliver the material. There are four traditional methods for preparing information for presentation: memory, manuscript (read), impromptu, and extemporaneous (Sandford and Yeager 1942).

   I. Money is always needed to start a small business.
      A. The most common way small businesses are financed is by owners tapping into their personal savings.
      B. The next best way to get the business financed is by selling off some of the ownership in the business for cash.
  II. The small business owner needs to know where the business will be located.
      A. A poor location can starve a small business into bankruptcy.
      B. A very good location can help even a mediocre business stay afloat.
 III. The small business owner will need to know if licensures or permits are required.
      A. In cases where food and alcoholic beverages are sold, permits and licensures from cities and states where the businesses will be located are required.
      B. Failing to procure a license can mean the business is breaking laws and owners can be fined or worse, the city could force the small business to be closed!
 IV. The small business owner needs to know who the customers will be.
      A. The main reason small businesses fail is they have no customers.
      B. Failing to understand the needs and desires of people who will be patrons of the business is a typical error of small business start-ups.
  V. The small business owner will need to spend a lot of money on marketing in the first year.
      A. An affordable marketing strategy needs to be developed first.
      B. Once a marketing strategy is developed a marketing plan can be developed.
         1. A marketing plan includes a strategy for segmenting customers.
         2. A marketing plan includes having a target of customers within a segment.
            a. Once a customer group is targeted, the marketing mix can be designed specifically to meet the needs of that group.
            b. The plan should be suitable for the targeted customers.
Closing: The closing can be a: summary, questions, story or anecdote, quotations, alternative, dramatic, action, incentive, fear, or conscience-pricking (Stanton 2009).

Figure 1.2 A formal sentence outline for a presentation on starting a small business

Types of Presentations

The *memory method* is used for a presentation memorized word-for-word and committed totally to memory. The danger of forgetting information is a disadvantage of the memory method. When you try to memorize an entire presentation, forgetting key parts will lead to problems. Skipping key parts of the presentation make it difficult to get back on track. Managers who memorize their presentations will often find themselves at a loss when they forget key parts due to distractions or interruptions. Adjusting to the audience's needs is also difficult with a memorized delivery. However, when you need to recite information, it may be good to memorize it first.

The *manuscript method* involves writing out your presentation and reading it to your audience, sometimes with the help of a teleprompter. Normally dignitaries, prime ministers, presidents of nations, and other high-level diplomats and political leaders use this method, because it allows for careful word choice with a lesser chance of forgetting information or inserting an errant word. For example, when the president of the United States speaks on the subject of aggression toward nations in the Middle East, it can have serious effects on how those nations view the United States. Words are carefully chosen in advance, and there can be no variation in the content. Misstatements can lead to disastrous results.

The *impromptu method* applies to casual conversations in business meetings and to more relaxed presentation situations. Holding a question-and-answer session after a planned presentation is an application of this method. The impromptu method is characterized by unscripted delivery. This does not mean that the presenter is unprepared. In fact, good speakers are always prepared, should the opportunity arise.

Impromptu speakers rely on their bank of knowledge and the use of commonly known arguments, or stock arguments, to add flavor and interest to their presentation.

The *extemporaneous method* involves the use of a formal outline, a defined purpose, detailed research, and organized MP and SP. The speech is delivered conversationally and naturally with enthusiasm and poise. It is the most commonly used presentation method in business and is the most effective method for achieving a persuasive purpose. It typically begins with an outline that includes main ideas and subordinate ideas, and it requires multiple practice sessions to enhance both vocal and nonverbal delivery skills. Although the main ideas are committed to memory, the presentation is not a word-for-word delivery. The speaker is free to use spontaneous words and phrases for a more conversational delivery and maximum flexibility.

The *elevator presentation* is the name given to very short presentations that can be delivered in the time required for a typical elevator ride. Usually, 30 seconds to 1 minute in length, elevator presentations contain all the elements of an effective oral presentation and are delivered in close proximity to a small captive audience. Since the average rate of speech for most Americans is 130 to 150 words per minute, the total words in the presentation should be planned accordingly. Preparing the elevator presentation in advance should not take away the conversational quality of the delivery. The audience normally will be one or a few persons who can influence an important decision affecting the presenter. The action-oriented elevator presentation means that you will need to know clearly your persuasive intent. Though you should not memorize the presentation, practice thoroughly and be prepared to discuss fully your main ideas or selling points, should the opportunity arise.

Delivery

The delivery of your presentation is what the audience sees, hears, and what ultimately determines if your message is believable. A good delivery makes for an effective presentation and includes both vocal and nonverbal cues. Practicing both elements of your presentation is fundamental to a good delivery. When practicing, do not stop each time you think you have made a mistake; instead, keep going, and take mental notes as you progress. Practice in increments of 30 minutes. If you have 3 hours to practice, divide that time into six separate sessions.

Delivery is fundamental because no amount of preparation, content, planning will overcome poor delivery skills. Window into Practical Reality 1.1 relates one of the most important speeches in history; one that asked soldiers in World War II to give their lives on behalf of their country.

Window into Practical Reality 1.1

General Patton's 1944 Normandy Invasion Speech

Men, this stuff some sources sling around about America wanting to stay out of the war and not wanting to fight is a lot of baloney! Americans love to fight, traditionally. All real Americans love the sting and clash of battle. America loves a winner. America will not tolerate a loser. Americans despise a coward; Americans play to win. That's why America has never lost and never will lose a war.

You are not all going to die. Only 2 percent of you, right here today, would be killed in a major battle.

Death must not be feared. Death, in time, comes to all of us. And every man is scared in his first action. If he says he's not, he's a goddamn liar. Some men are cowards, yes, but they fight just the same, or get the hell slammed out of them.

The real hero is the man who fights even though he's scared. Some get over their fright in a minute, under fire; others take an hour; for some it takes days; but a real man will never let the fear of death overpower his honor, his sense of duty, to his country and to his manhood.

All through your Army careers, you've been bitching about what you call "chicken-shit drills." That, like everything else in the Army, has a definite purpose. That purpose is instant obedience to orders and to create and maintain constant alertness! This must be bred into every soldier. A man must be alert all the time if he expects to stay alive. If not, some German son-of-a-bitch will sneak up behind him with a sock full of shit! There are 400 neatly marked graves somewhere in Sicily, all because one man went to sleep on his job—but they are German graves, because we caught the bastards asleep!

An Army is a team, lives, sleeps, fights, and eats as a team. This individual hero stuff is a lot of horse shit! The bilious bastards who write that kind of stuff for the *Saturday Evening Post* don't know any more about real fighting under fire than they know about f**king! Every single man in the Army plays a vital role. Every man has his job to do and must do it. What if every truck driver decided that he didn't like the whine of a shell overhead, turned yellow and jumped headlong into a ditch? What if every man thought, "They won't miss me, just one in millions?" Where in Hell would we be now? Where would our country, our loved ones, our homes, even the world, be?

No, thank God, Americans don't think like that. Every man does his job, serves the whole. Ordnance men supply and maintain the guns and vast machinery of this war, to keep us rolling. Quartermasters bring up clothes and food, for where we're going, there isn't a hell of a lot to steal. Every last man on KP has a job to do, even the guy who boils the water to keep us from getting the GI shits!

Remember, men, you don't know I'm here. No mention of that is to be made in any letters. The United States is supposed to be wondering what the hell has happened to me. I'm not supposed to be commanding this Army, I'm not supposed even to be in England. Let the first bastards to find out be the goddamn Germans. I want them to look up and howl, "Ach, it's the goddamn Third Army and that son-of-a-bitch Patton again!"

We want to get this thing over and get the hell out of here, and get at those purple-pissin' Japs!!! The shortest road home is through Berlin and Tokyo! We'll win this war, but we'll win it only by showing the enemy we have more guts than they have or ever will have!

There's one great thing you men can say when it's all over and you're home once more. You can thank God that 20 years from now, when you're sitting around the fireside with your grandson on your knee and he asks you what you did in the war, you won't have to shift him to the other knee, cough, and say, "I shoveled shit in Louisiana."

Source: www.speeches-usa.com.

General George S. Patton's speech "Invasion of Normandy" was a final *pep talk* delivered to his troops on May 17, 1944. It is the prototypical persuasive speech to stir the audience to immediate action, and Patton's delivery was key. We are sure that General Patton thought about what he was going to say, but he did not deliver this as a written speech but as an extemporaneous speech with no notes!

A presenter such as General Patton will also look for cues that the audience has received and interpreted the encoded message correctly. The speaker must interpret those cues from observations while presenting. The audience will send the source an encoded message in the form of applause, nodding, eye contact, and so on. This nonverbal body language is feedback about the audiences' understanding of the message and will help the speaker to make the necessary adjustments.

Proper understanding by the audience is crucial, if your presentations are to achieve your intended purpose. You will refine your message throughout your presentation based on receiving and responding to verbal and nonverbal cues from your audience. Extraneous sidebar conversations, restlessness, and nodding are good indications that you should immediately shift to a more appropriate tone, pitch, topic, or delivery method.

Speech Dangers and Filled Pauses

Eye contact with the audience is essential to giving an effective presentation, as it engages individuals and causes them to feel that you are talking directly to them. Most people will form their impressions about the presenter within about a minute, and effective eye contact is key to making a favorable impression.

Nervous speech and actions early in your presentation can lead to a negative first impression on your audience. These distractions that generally happen at the beginning of a presentation are caused by the speaker's nervousness and the accompanying adrenalin rush. Many times we are not even aware of our nonverbal habits (McKenzie 2002). A great idea is to have someone video record you while you are giving a presentation, then critique it with someone you respect. Watch the audience as well as yourself to gauge the effectiveness of your presentation.

Observing the body language of your audience can reveal much about their acceptance of your ideas. If they are shuffling their feet, furrowing their brow, or not looking at you, they are probably not following you. In response to a controversial topic, audience members may grimace, turn their head and upper torso away from you, clench their teeth, or take a confrontational stance such as putting their hands on their hips.

Recognition of body language is very important for the audience to understand what the speaker is saying, but also so the speaker understands what the audience is receiving or rejecting.

Bender (1991) and Detz (2007) each presented 12 solutions to better enable managers to deliver effective presentations. In Table 1.2, note the similarities of each authors' views concerning the elements of effective presentations. Detz (2014) offers a plethora of good delivery tips in her recent book titled, *How to Write & Give a Speech*.

Table 1.2 Tips from Bender and Detz for improving the oral presentation

Bender (1991) offers 12 tips on making powerful presentations	Detz (2007) offers 12 tips to help improve the oral presentation
1. Touch the audience's emotions.	1. Focus your topic.
2. Move the audience to action.	2. Analyze your audience.
3. Use familiar language to build rapport and trust.	3. Use interesting research.
4. Use shorter words and phrases.	4. Organize your material.
5. Maintain an idea file.	5. Use simple language.
6. Keep the structure as simple as possible.	6. Give your presentation some style.
7. Monitor the reaction of the audience.	7. Use a light touch of humor.
8. Make the audience participants, rather than just spectators.	8. Practice your delivery.
9. Use an unusual statistic.	9. Consider your "vocal personality."
10. Make a realistic promise and follow through.	10. Use body language that reinforces your words.
11. Show a short video or use an overhead transparency.	11. Get good media coverage.
12. Vary the voice.	12. Evaluate the merits of each speaking invitation.

Source: www.PeterUrsBender.com.

Effective oral presentations do not have to be perfect, but presenters must be prepared. Figure 1.3 provides a convenient list of executive oral presentations missteps and solutions for those missteps (Bates 2007).

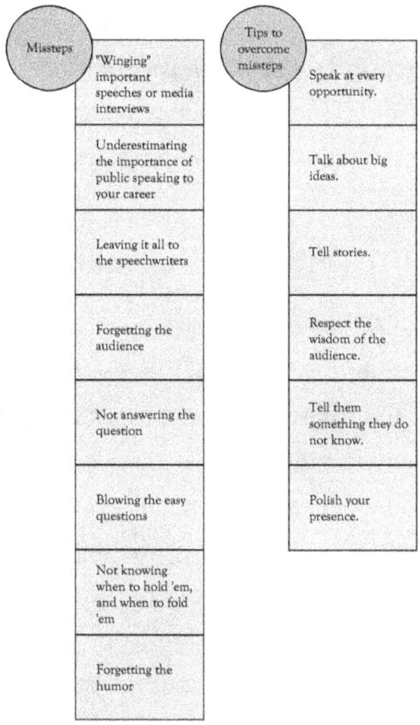

Figure 1.3 Missteps and solutions to common problems in executive presentations

Filled pauses (FP) refer to a situation in which the presenter uses repetitious, irrelevant words or phrases without being consciously aware it is happening. Examples of fillers include um, uh, like, you see, or any other repetitive word or sound. Howell and Sackin (2001) argue that using FP in abundance contributes to what they call "fluency failure" in recognized speech. In a very interesting article, Schachter and others (1991) referred to the "agrammatical" use of FP among university lecturers as "disfluency." Speakers appear to be uncertain and lack confidence when using needless repetitious words or phrases in abundance to fill pauses. In addition, it breaks the audience's attention.

One study of communication behaviors showed that females engaged in more justifiers, intensifiers, and agreement than males; whereas, males engaged in more vocalized pauses and also received more vocalized pauses than females (Turner and Dindia 1995). To eliminate FP from your oral presentation requires three steps (1) learn to hear yourself using FP by undergoing some type of sensitivity training, such as recording and critiquing your presentations or having an expert critique with you; (2) practice FP reduction by paying close attention to its usage—create a cognitive transformation; and (3) practice being silent each time a pause is required for grammar, emphasis, and mental deliberation (Bell 2011).

Presenting with Emotions

Audiences are turned off when presenters lack emotions. Emotions are a part of any delivery, including business presentations. Being excited about your presentation is the surest way to exude emotion while presenting.

Too often, presenters fail to understand that their single most important job is to convey facts and ideas in a way that the audience will understand the benefits in an engaging manner. A *humdrum talker* delivers presentations in a monotone voice, and this type of behavior will more than guarantee an in-kind reaction from your audience. People resent presenters who lack enthusiasm, strong feelings, or sincerity in their presentation.

Sincerity is a quality that reflects an honest attempt to reach the audience and achieve the identified purpose. If listeners find a speaker to be sincere, they will trust and follow. Sincerity includes the qualities of honesty and passion for the topic. Emotions that are sincere and honest will help you connect with your audience.

What makes one person a better presenter than another? If two people are intellectual equals, why would they not be equally effective speakers? If both speakers read and applied the same tips, you would think both presentations would be equally impressive. However, we are not all created equal in every respect. In recent years, attention has focused on measures of intelligence that go beyond traditional "cognitive" or "school ready" indicators. Newer measures focus on verbal/linguistic, logical/mathematical, musical, visual/spatial, body/kinesthetic, interpersonal, and intrapersonal (Gardner 1993).

Emotional intelligence is the ability to read others and respond in a way that matches their emotional reaction. Five identified domains of emotional intelligence include (1) knowing your own emotions, (2) managing your emotions, (3) motivating yourself, (4) recognizing emotions in others, and (5) handling relationships. While all five domains are applicable to delivering effective oral presentations, recognizing and managing your own feelings and those of others are key aspects of effective delivery. Smart people can appear socially and emotionally inept when they do not interpret their own and others' emotions correctly. On the other hand, people who are emotionally intelligent know their true emotions, practice to control and manage fierce emotions, remain motivated by gaining control over their emotions, anticipate and balance theirs and others' emotions, and foster fruitful relationships by communicating intelligently (Goleman 1995).

Persuasive Patterns Using Figures of Speech

Throughout history, a few remarkable leaders have demonstrated such amazing oratory powers that they were able to convince an entire nation to follow them. These incredibly gifted speakers used stylistic touches as vehicles by which they drove their messages home, convincing people to change both their beliefs and actions. A speaker deliberately uses *figures of speech* to raise language from the ordinary to a level of heightened intensity to further appeal to the audience emotionally. The speaker can appeal to the audience through their reasoning skills, through their emotions, by offering them a sense of urgency, or by appearing to have credibility as the speaker—as someone who knows.

Patrick Henry's "Liberty or Death" presentation is such an example. Evoking emotion was the intent of his hammered down and chiseled stylistic words. Like a chef's blade, Henry's words sliced deep into the widely held truths and helped lawmakers see that young America's independence could only be achieved through defiance of tyrannical control. There can be no doubt Henry's purpose was to persuade lawmakers to take immediate action toward inevitable war. The resistance of the colonies to the attempts of England to tax them culminated in the Boston Tea Party of December 16, 1773, which resulted in the closing of the Port of Boston to British ships. The phrase "Liberty or Death" stands as a timeless antithesis and as an impassioned hyperbole. Henry was able to paint vivid, colorful pictures of inevitable doom as a certain result of American complacency. He skillfully used irony and antithesis to forge extreme psychic images of gloom for inaction and splendor of independence for immediate action.

His phrase, "for my own part, I consider it as nothing less than a question of freedom or slavery" (Parrish and Murphy 1947, p. 35) captured the thrust of his central thought.

Window into Practical Reality 1.2 illustrates another masterful use of speech by U.S. President Franklin D. Roosevelt (FDR) in his state of war address on the occasion of the United States entry into World War II.

Window into Practical Reality 1.2

Franklin D. Roosevelt, December 8, 1941 (FDR) Declares "A State of War" against Japan

Yesterday, December 7, 1941—(a) a date which will live in infamy—the (b) United States of America was suddenly and deliberately attacked by naval and air forces of the empire of Japan.

The United States was at peace with that nation, and, at the solicitation of Japan, was still in conversation with its government and its Emperor looking toward the maintenance of peace in the Pacific.

(c) Indeed, 1 hour after Japanese air squadrons had commenced bombing in the American island of Oahu, the Japanese Ambassador to the United States and his colleague delivered to our Secretary of State a formal reply to a recent American message. While this reply stated that it seemed useless to continue the existing diplomatic negotiations, it contained no threat or hint of war or armed attack.

It will be recorded that the distance of Hawaii from Japan makes it obvious that the attack was deliberately planned many days or even weeks ago. During the intervening time the Japanese government has deliberately sought to deceive the United States by false statements and expressions of hope for continued peace.

The attack yesterday on the Hawaiian Islands has caused severe damage to American naval and military forces. I regret to tell you that very many Americans lives have been lost. In addition, American ships have been reported torpedoed on the high seas between San Francisco and Honolulu.

Yesterday the Japanese government also launched an attack against Malaya.

Last night Japanese forces attacked Hong Kong.

Last night Japanese forces attacked Guam.

Last night Japanese forces attacked the Philippine Islands.

(d) Last night the Japanese attacked Wake Island.

And this morning the Japanese attacked Midway Island.

Japan has therefore undertaken a surprise offensive extending throughout the Pacific area. The facts of yesterday and today speak for themselves. The people of the United States have already formed their opinions, and well understand the implications to the very life and safety of our nation.

As Commander-in-Chief of the Army and Navy, I have directed that all measures be taken for our defense.

Always will we remember the character of the onslaught against us. No matter how long it may take us to overcome this premeditated invasion, the American people, in their righteous might, will win through to absolute victory. I believe I interpret the will of the Congress and of the people when I assert that we will not only defend ourselves to the uttermost but will make very certain that this form of treachery shall never again endanger us.

Hostilities exist. There is no blinking at the fact that our people, our territory, and our interests are in grave danger.

With confidence in our armed forces, with the unbounding determination of our people, we will gain the inevitable triumph, so help us God.

(e) I ask that the Congress declare that, since the unprovoked and dastardly attack by Japan on Sunday, December 7, 1941, a state of war has existed between the United States and the Japanese Empire.

FDR delivered his moving presentation to the nation and Congress the day after the Pearl Harbor attack. Needing the permission from Congress to declare war on Japan, FDR went to the people to get the necessary support. You can clearly see the power of figures of speech in FDR's address. He uses (a) *personification,* an attribution of personal form, character, or representation of a thing or abstraction as a person. He uses (b) *synecdoche,* a part is put for the whole or the whole for a part.

He uses (c) *antithesis*, the contrasting of words, as when placed at the beginning and end of a single sentence or clause. He uses (d) *tautology*, repetition of the same words or use of synonymous words in close succession. He uses (e) *interrogation-rhetorical question,* a question not intended to elicit an answer, where the answer is understood.

Window into Practical Reality 1.3 illustrates how the mainstream media often uses hyperbole or litotes to heighten or lessen emotions among the masses, by framing a narrative on a particular issue, in order to gain consensus from the public on a particular point of view.

Window into Practical Reality 1.3

"Pigs in a Blanket—Fry Like Bacon!"

On July 7, 2016, in Dallas, Texas, a sniper attack led to five police officers being killed. It is among the most tragic situations in American history concerning police officers and the public. The media was partially to blame for hyping up the emotions among African Americans with their hyperbolic portrayal of the facts on police shootings of Black people in America. The media, it seems, deliberately used hyperbole to inflame the public, fostered credibility onto Black Lives Matter (BLM), and undermined the public's trust of the police. The media used strong language, exaggerated statistics (making gross generalizations from isolated situations with no due process for the police officers involved), and put into the public's imagination images of the fatalities between the police and Black people as malice aforethought on the part of the police. However, the media could have simply reported the facts without editorializing, and perhaps had they done so, the five Dallas police officers might still be alive. The media knows, unfortunately, that emotionally bland, dull coverage offers little appeal for the viewing public.

For example, according to the Department of Justice, Bureau of Justice Statistics for 2017, there were 987 fatalities caused by the police, of which 223 were Black people. Despite knowing that the police kill more White people each year in America than Black people,

(Rankin 2018) reports the information this way: "223 Black people were shot and killed by police (23 percent of all shootings, despite accounting for 13.3 percent of the population); that is 10 fewer than in 2016." Rankin's use of hyperbole and exaggerated statistics is to imply bias and malice among police toward Black people. Rankin failed to report that more than half the police caused fatalities were White people. However, there are multiple ways media could have reported the same data.

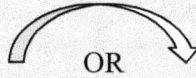

OR

Hyperbole is the exaggerated use of words or phrases which takes visual language beyond the realms of reality, physical or psychological (i.e., Your father put an ocean of icing on that cake! I'm as mad as hell!). Opposite of litotes.	Litotes is the denial of its opposite by plainly stating the obvious (i.e., You know that $30 million dollar lottery you just won is no small amount of money.). Opposite of hyperbole.
Hyperbolic Narrative in Media Tonight, there has been another shooting of a young Black man at the hands of the police. Last year in 2017, there were 223 Black people killed by police, that's one Black person killed by the police every 39 hours in America in 2017, and 94 of these Black victims were unarmed. Too often, a police officer who kills an unarmed Black person will never be brought to justice. Rarely are police punished for their crimes. We must ask ourselves a question in these circumstances, do Black lives matter?	**Litotes Narrative in Media** It is very tragic for any person to lose his or her life at the hands of the police; nevertheless, we must grant all police officers the due process that any other American citizen deserves. We must examine all the facts and allow the police officer a fair hearing before we make a rush-to-judgment. Let us all keep in mind that there are 21.5 million Black males in America. Police encounter millions of Black people every year and rarely do these encounters lead to a fatality between a Black person and the police. The 223 fatalities in 2017 among 21.5 million Black males in the population, assures us that the odds of a Black male being killed by a police officer is extremely small. In all 223 fatalities, the cases were thoroughly investigated, and when an officer was guilty of a crime that officer was prosecuted and punished.

Using Charts, Graphs, and Tables

Visual aids often are beneficial to the effectiveness of the presentation and to conveying persuasive meanings. Body movement, eye contact, facial expression, mechanical devices, color usage in slides, electronic equipment (including PowerPoint or Prezi), and nontechnical devices (flip chart, chalkboard, transparency, etc.) are all examples of visual aids used to enhance the effectiveness of a presentation. The media you choose should fit the type of presentation you are giving. Different media will help you achieve different results. In addition, different media help different learners with their comprehension and learning of what you are speaking about.

Visual messages help reinforce the verbal message, which shifts an audience's beliefs and actions toward the presenter's purpose. Furthermore, people learn by hearing, seeing, and doing so engaging the audience is important. Visual messages are also important to decision making and analysis as they help guide the users through the decision-making process. The old saying, "a picture is worth 10,000 words," can be very true. But it is also true that too many graphics can make for a cluttered message.

Charts and graphs are types of visual aids that help convey meaning. Six variations of charts can help you convey your presentation message; these include pie charts, bar charts, line charts, area charts, pictograms, and tables.

Pie charts compare parts of a whole or pieces of a pie. A slice represents a portion of the whole, for example, total sales by quarter. The whole pie represents the total sales for a given year. Chart 1.1 illustrates the quarterly percent of sales for four-quarters.

Note that each quarter's sales is shown as a proportionate or percentage slice. The percentages must equal 100 percent, and the starting point of a pie chart is 12:00 noon. Pie charts should not be presented in 3D as this distorts the graph.

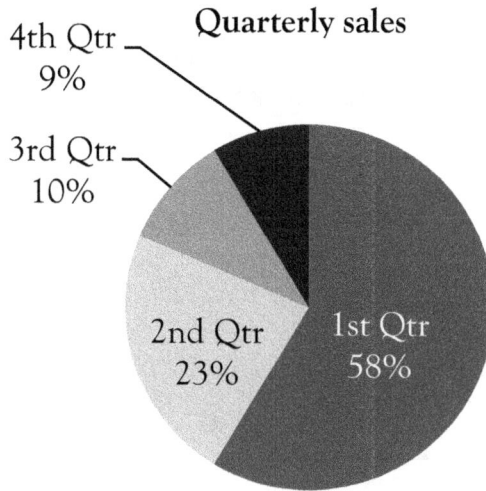

Chart 1.1 *Use of a pie chart to depict quarterly sales*

Bar charts, also known as column charts, compare or correlate data. Chart 1.2 illustrates a correlation of consumption of soybeans, wheat, and corn for four-quarters of a year.

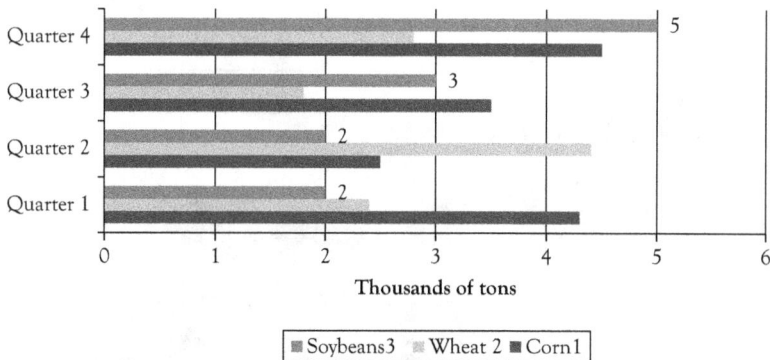

Chart 1.2 *Use of a bar chart (column chart) for comparing crop production*

A bar chart may be oriented horizontally or vertically, and both axes must be labeled clearly. Numbers may be shown at the top or end of the columns to mitigate any difficulty in interpreting each bar's value. Again, 3D distorts these graphs and should not be used.

Line graphs compare time series data or frequency data. Line graphs show relative differences in quantities or changes in value over time, for example, enrollment trends among three business schools over a 3-year period. Chart 1.3 illustrates quarterly trends for the hypothetical quantities of soybeans, wheat, and corn sold in a year.

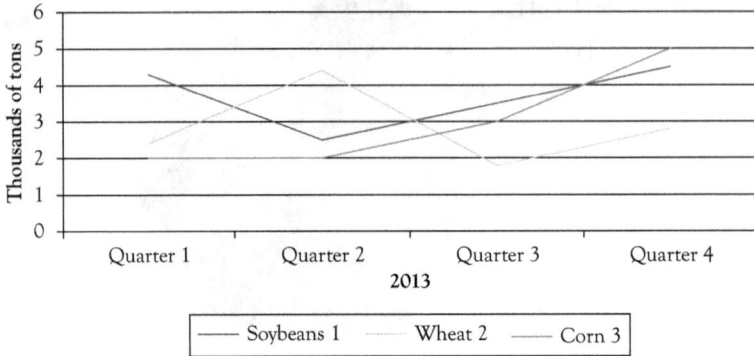

Chart 1.3 Use of a line chart to depict multiple crop trends

Area graphs compare geographic, spatial, or time data. Chart 1.4 illustrates a hypothetical comparison of the population of people facing starvation in a less developed country, and its correlation with economic prosperity in the United States.

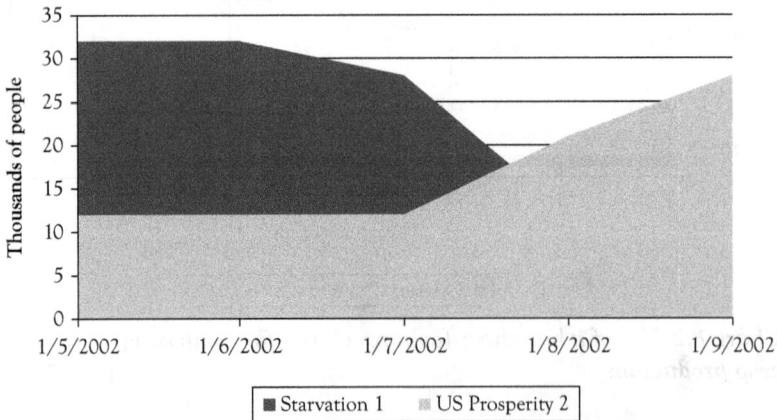

Chart 1.4 Use of an area chart to compare a less developed country starvation with U.S. prosperity

By using quantitative comparison and contrasting colors, Chart 1.4 depicts an inverse relationship between the starvation in the less developed country and the economic progress in the United States.

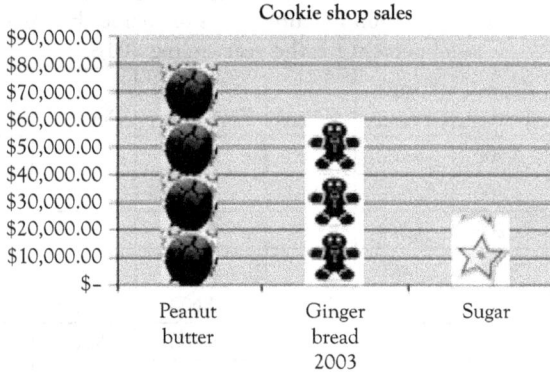

Chart 1.5 Use of a pictogram to compare sales of three products
Source: Creating Pictographs (2010).

Pictograms are much like pie charts or bar graphs; however, they use icons to exemplify the differences between the elements. Chart 1.5 illustrates the difference in cookie shop sales for peanut butter, ginger bread, and sugar cookies.

Managers use tables to report results for complex information that would require an unnecessary amount of written text to communicate. Chart 1.6 illustrates a hypothetical example of in-store sales for peanut butter, ginger bread, and sugar cookies at five different store locations.

The table data include actual sales of each type of cookie and the total sales, per location. Each location's sales percentage, in proportion to the total sales of all five locations, is also shown. While Chart 1.6 emphasizes store location, Chart 1.7 emphasizes the types of cookies sold.

Frequency information and percentages will help your managerial decision making. For example, if a type of cookie should represent at least 10 percent of sales for all five store locations combined, Chart 1.6 is much better at helping you determine which cookie type must be eliminated at particular store locations. In our example, location three should not sell sugar cookies, and location five should not sell peanut butter and ginger bread cookies. On the other hand, Chart 1.7 illustrates that for in-store sales, peanut butter cookies are problematic for location 5 only if the criterion is that a cookie type should represent 10 percent of total sales for a single store location.

Stores	Peanut butter	Ginger bread	Sugar	Frequency	Percent	Cumulative percent
In-store sales by location for three types of cookies by frequency and percent for the year ending 2018						
Location 1	2,200	3,000	1,500	6,700	23.8	23.8
Location 2	1,800	2,800	1,800	6,400	22.7	46.5
Location 3	1,200	1,200	300	2,700	9.6	56.1
Location 4	3,000	2,800	3,000	8,800	31.2	87.3
Location 5	200	500	2,900	3,600	12.8	100.0
Total	8,400	10,300	9,500	28,200	100	
	Percent	Percent	Percent			
Location 1	26.2	29.1	15.8			
Location 2	21.4	27.2	18.9			
Location 3	14.3	11.7	3.2			
Location 4	35.7	27.2	31.6			
Location 5	2.4	4.9	30.5			

Chart 1.6 *Frequency and percent of sales by store locations in table form*

Cookies	Location 1	Location 2	Location 3	Location 4	Location 5	Frequency	Percent	Cumulative percent
In-store sales by cookies for three types of cookies by frequency and percent for the year ending 2018								
Peanut butter	2,200	1,800	1,200	3,000	200	8,400	29.8	29.8
Ginger bread	3,000	2,800	1,200	2,800	500	10,300	36.5	66.3
Sugar	1,500	1,800	300	3,000	2,900	9,500	33.7	100.0
Total	6,700	6,400	2,700	8,800	3,600	28,200	100.0	
	Percent	Percent	Percent	Percent	Percent			
Peanut butter	32.8	28.1	44.4	34.1	5.6			
Ginger bread	44.8	43.8	44.4	31.8	13.9			
Sugar	22.4	28.1	11.1	34.1	80.6			

Chart 1.7 *Frequency and percent of sales by cookie sales in table form*

Following a few commonsense rules will aid you in the design of effective graphics. Choose themes and slide design to match the subject or occasion and use complimentary background and foreground colors. Be sure that red, blue, and green colors do not touch each other because color-blind people cannot see differences between the colors. Limit the number of visuals in your presentation with only one idea per slide and limit each slide to one idea. Make sure text labels in graphics are large enough to be easily read by the audience.

Be aware that graphics can be used for unethical purposes. Graphics can be used to support a lie or to stretch the truth. It is important when making graphics to be sure that the proportions are correct. The "three-quarter high" is a rule-of-thumb stating that the emphasis of any graph should be on the x-axis—horizontal axis (width), thus, the y-axis—vertical (height) of the graph should be three-fourths the length of the x-axis. Ensure that the axes, bars, and pies are all labeled completely to provide the audience a full understanding of the graphic without a verbal explanation. It is also always important to explain in words exactly what the graphic shows, unless it is easily apparent. The graphic should be sandwiched between the introduction of the graphic and the explanation of the graphic.

Summary

In effective oral presentations, the presenter selects and accomplishes the intended *purpose.* Second, effective oral presentation requires adequate *preparation.* Third, effective oral presentation incorporates good vocal and bodily *delivery.* Possible objectives for a presentation include belief, action, narrative, descriptive, explanation, and gratification.

The general styles for presentation delivery are memory, manuscript (read), impromptu, and extemporaneous. The elevator presentation is a special type of extemporaneous presentation that is short and to the point. Practicing your presentation, regardless of delivery style, is fundamental to success.

The introduction, body, and conclusion are the three main portions of a presentation. The introduction's function is to tell them what you will tell them, the body's function is to tell them, and the conclusion's function is to tell them what you just told them.

A filled pause is any overused, meaningless sound or phrase that results when a nervous speaker tries to fill the silent void. Effective speakers recognize their own filler tendencies and overcome the habit by pausing for emphasis or audience deliberation. Be aware of verbal techniques such as hyperbole often used to influence you emotionally, especially when the media is reporting on information of a sensational nature.

Emotions are feelings that the presentation elicits from both you as the presenter and your audience. Humdrum speakers elicit boredom and irritability from their audiences. Sincerity is perceived by the audience as an honest attempt to connect and achieve your speaking purpose. Studying the patterns of speech of great presentations can be helpful in learning how to inspire and change peoples' points of view. Various types of charts and graphs are visual aids to help convey meaning and clarity for your presentation message.

CHAPTER 2

Impression Management

Objectives

After reading this chapter, you will be able to:

1. delineate the nuances of impression management theory;
2. describe the specifics of nonverbal impression management;
3. explain how your dress, behavior, and personal environment influence impressions;
4. explain how you can use impression management to manage others.

Introduction

Those selfies you take may give strangers odd impressions of you. Most people under the age of 30 and many over that take selfies. However, these people are seen by strangers as more negative, less trustworthy, less socially attractive, less open to new experiences, more narcissistic, and more extroverted than the same person in photos taken by others, either alone or in a group. People are seen as more attractive when they are in photos with others (Kramer et al. 2017). Though you cannot control or predict the impression that you make through selfies, you are, nevertheless, making an impression. You must be careful of what you put online that others can see, whether you are at work or even on your personal time.

Celebrities manage the impressions they portray by what they purchase, what they wear, what they do to their bodies, and how they present themselves to the public. Some celebrities' attempts at self-presentation can be ridiculous. Guyism.com listed the top 10 ridiculous celebrity purchases, ranging from an $850 purse for Suri Cruise (just a child), Michael Vick's $85,000 fish pond, Beyonce's $100,000 pair of leggings, to Rachel Hunter's $15,000 doghouse (Guyism 2013). Although these purchases may seem extreme for ordinary people, celebrities know that the right kind of image portrayed to the public can be lucrative and make them appear irresistible.

Another example of this obsession with celebrity image is the $32,000 appearance fee paid to Snooki from *Jersey Shore* by Rutgers University, which was $2,000 more than the amount Rutgers paid famed Nobel Laureate, Toni Morrison, for an appearance (Larkin 2017)! Even though outrage followed Snooki's visit, why do you suppose the Rutgers University Programming Association was willing to pay Snooki that kind of fee? Why do we know about Suri Cruise's purse in the first place? Is it accidental or deliberate that we know these seemingly unimportant facts? Why do we care about Beyonce's leggings? Why do ordinary people live beyond their means, drive cars they cannot afford, purchase homes out of their price range, or adorn their bodies with expensive suits they do not truly like?

In his seminal analysis, Goffman (1959) captured the essence of what celebrities and common people are trying to achieve through their attempts at being noticed. Goffman described what people do in public as akin to a theatrical performance. Individuals act on a daily basis in a manner that will create a desirable public image among their peers. Individuals in everyday life use expressive personal items to enhance their persona. Goffman also believed that when individuals are outside the public's view, on a hypothetical backstage, they can be themselves and shed their public personas.

Managers, too, use impressionistic behavior to enhance the effectiveness of their leadership. If an upper-management person breaks a social contract with an employee, the trust the person had created will be destroyed and the employee will become very cynical (James and Shaw 2016). There are a variety of impression management qualities (verbal and nonverbal, dress, environment, and so on) within the broader framework of managerial communication. The impression you make every day at work affects your credibility with those above, equal to, and below you in the organization. An impression is very difficult to change and that is why first impressions are important. While we typically form an impression of someone in less than a minute, it could take years to change that first impression.

Impression Management Theory

Some people in the corporate world deliberately try to cause others to see them in a particular way through staging or acting (Goffman 1959); however, everyone leaves an impression on others even if not intentionally. *Impression management* is concerned with the organization's or individual's attempt to influence the impression that others have of them (Nelson and Quick 2003). Impression management can include both verbal and nonverbal behaviors as well as physical appearance. *Symbolic interactionism theories* explain that individuals select and create their friendships and social activity environments to reinforce who they are—dispositions, preferences, attitudes, and self-image (Buss 1987; Snyder and Ickes 1985; Swann 1987). People decorate their personal and work spaces to fit their personal tastes. The personal materials are a direct reflection of the individual's personality and give the area a sense of identity. People base impressions on one's physical appearance such as skin tone, age, and hair; or on social roles such as professional, blue collar, or retired; and on their personal biases.

Research has shown that impression management is pervasive throughout organizations, and that there are risks and rewards of using the technique. Window into Practical Reality 2.1 illustrates the impression management experiences of two organizations, one which resulted in a positive response from the public and the other the opposite.

Assertive Strategies

A manager's use of *assertive strategies* can lead to images that are either desirable or undesirable. Five assertive strategies include (1) ingratiation, (2) self-promotion, (3) exemplification, (4) supplication, and (5) intimidation. Figure 2.1 illustrates the assertive strategies, associated behaviors, and their desired or undesired image outcomes.

Window into Practical Reality 2.1

Disney's Grand Illusion	Starbuck's Grand Disillusion
An example of a company that works hard to develop a favorable impression on their customers is Disney. All employees are called cast members, all of whom receive extensive training in scripting their performances for their audiences at the theme parks, hotels, and restaurants. Think about all of the characters and the detail that goes into their clothing. Then remember the detail that goes into the rides in the theme parks. You will see cast members smiling a great deal because that makes the customers think Disney World is a happy place.	In 2015 the then CEO of Starbucks, Howard Schultz, went out on a limb against internal opposition and asked all the Baristas at every Starbucks restaurant in the country to engage in conversations with willing customers about race. In fact, Baristas went as far as to write on their coffee cups, "race together," in a beautiful cursive style of penmanship. On March 22, 2015, just one week after the marketing campaign started it ended in a complete disaster (Claveria 2015).
If you have ever been to Disney World in Orlando, Florida, or another of the Disney theme parks, you are certain to have witnessed firsthand the effect of this grand illusion on children—as they squirm to be first to hug Mickey when he appears!	Trolls and critics roasted Starbucks executives with ridicule and condemnation about the arrogance of Starbucks wanting to discuss sensitive cultural issues with strangers. It became quickly apparent to Starbucks' leadership team that people did not feel on any level that Starbucks was the right environment to engage in discussions on race relations in America. For one week, race together was worse than "New Coke!"

- Why has Disney's assertive strategy continued to be successful for so many decades?
- Which type of assertive strategy did Starbucks attempt to use, but failed to accomplish? Why did it fail?
- Was it possible the public reacted negatively to Starbuck's "race together" campaign because they saw it as artificial, self-serving, or conceited?

An ingratiating person is one who frequently compliments people without any real reason for doing so. *Ingratiation* as a strategy may be effective at times. For example, it has been found to positively influence performance evaluations and individual likeability (Kacmar and Carlson 1999; Seiter 2007), though effectiveness is influenced by the type of ingratiation tactic used, its transparency, and with whom it is used (Gordon 1996). Ingratiation is risky because it is so transparent, and for it to work effectively it must be subtle and not obvious. If the person it is being used on becomes suspicious, he or she will not believe the ingratiator (Potter 2014).

Assertive strategy— ingratiation Behavior: Flattery, favor-doing Desired image: Likeable Undesired image: Self-serving	Assertive strategy— self-promotion Behavior: Performance claims, boasting Desired image: Competent Undesired image: Conceited

Assertive strategy—exemplification Behavior: Going beyond call of duty, appearing busy Desired image: Dedicated Undesired image: Feels superior

Assertive strategy— supplication Behavior: Asking for help, playing dumb Desired image: Needy Undesired image: Lazy	Assertive strategy— intimidation Behavior: Making threats, displaying anger Desired image: Intimidating Undesired image: Bossy

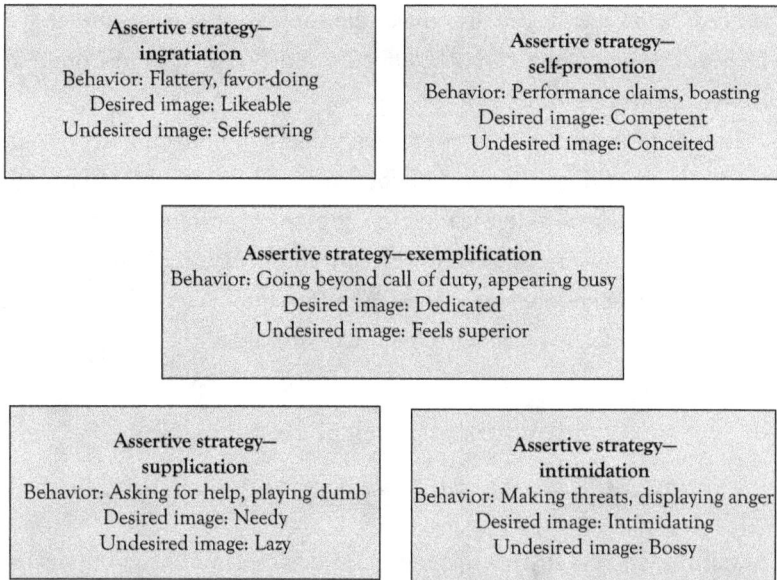

Figure 2.1 Five assertive strategies for impression management and image outcomes

Source: Crane and Crane (2002, p. 28).

Self-promotion includes boasting about one's work in an attempt to positively impact others. When an organization engages in self-promotion, it normally does this in the form of what marketers call "puffery," that is the best burger in town, or you will never have a better night's sleep. However, you will want to be careful with boasts and not exaggerate; otherwise, others will tend to disregard your claims.

Because *exemplification* can be seen as going beyond what is required in one's job, it can be seen as positive by some, while others may view it as hypocritical and self-serving. People tend not to like those who have a superiority complex. When used properly by a manager, exemplification can be viewed by employees as indicating that the person is a worthy role model and an effective leader, who is a transformational force in the organization.

Using *supplication* as an impression management tool occurs when the user indicates that someone else is more qualified for a task or assignment. Most people enjoy having others look up to them, so this technique often works to the supplicant's advantage to get the resources he or she needs. However, it can also make the supplicant appear unqualified, which means that while it may be effective short term, it can be quite ineffective in the long run.

The use of *intimidation* is most often utilized in nonvoluntary or contractual relationships. The intimidator has the ability to inflict hardship on the recipient, such as in the military. The strategy can be effective when immediate action is necessary; however, in most organizations it leads to fear and distrust among recipients. Window into Practical Reality 2.2 illustrates the risks involved with the use of intimidation.

Window into Practical Reality 2.2

The Angry Waitress Makes an Impression

A waitress was very distressed when she did not get a sufficient tip from a dining group. As a result, she used a little intimidation for future diners by posting a picture and the story of the cheap tipper on YouTube for the world to see. Current U.S. employment and tax rules require restaurants and bars to pay an hourly rate of at least $2.13 per hour to wait staff and to report wages of at least $7.25 per hour, whether that proportion of tips is received or not. While some states require that a higher minimum wage be paid to servers, customers often do not realize that the hourly rate for a server is quite low. In other words, most servers would starve to death if all they received was their hourly rate.

- What do you suppose was the self-image of the waitress?
- By using an intimidation strategy, what do you suppose is the impression she has made on her future customers? What about her fellow servers?

Defensive Strategies

Managers can use *defensive strategies* in their impression management that can lead to both desirable and undesirable image outcomes. Five common defensive strategies include (1) innocence, (2) excuses, (3) justifications, (4) apologies, and (5) accounts (Gardner 1992; Gardner and Martinko 1988; Jones and Pittman 1982). Figure 2.2 illustrates these defensive strategies and their associated behaviors and desired or undesired image outcomes.

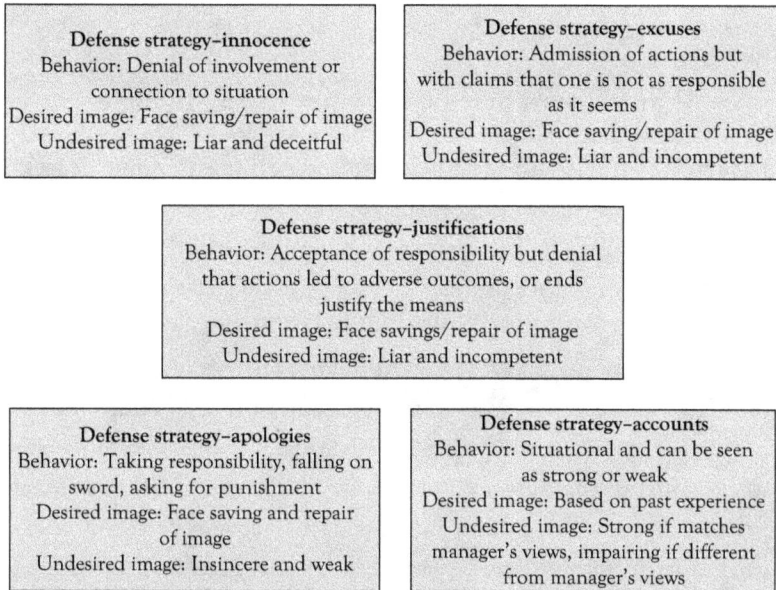

Figure 2.2 Five defensive strategies for impression management and image outcomes

Source: Crane and Crane (2002, p. 28).

Innocence, excuses, and justification all involve face-saving and an attempt to repair the image of the user; however, many times the receiver sees the person as a liar, deceitful, or incompetent. With the use of *innocence* (also called denial or refusal) the user denies responsibility, denies that the event occurred, blames others, or says that the blame cannot be apportioned.

The individual using an *excuse* tries to reduce responsibility by providing evidence that mitigates his or her responsibility for the actions that caused the situation.

Justification by the person responsible for the situation is an attempt to reduce the undesirability of the situation. In other words, the person accepts responsibility but denies the need for punishment. Window into Practical Reality 2.3 illustrates an example of ingratiation that went wrong for Paula Dean. Her justification that the incident happened a long time ago was seen as suspicious, and the media bias also did not help. Nevertheless, what happened to Paula Dean is a reflection of the images and expectations among the different race demographics in America.

Window into Practical Reality 2.3

Paula Dean and Discriminatory Language

In June 20, 2013, Paula Dean's empire fell apart due to someone leaking to the media the fact that, many years earlier, she had used language that showed a discriminatory bias. She admitted in a deposition for a lawsuit against her by a former manager at Dean's Savannah, Georgia, restaurant that she had used the "N-Word." The excuse that she had not used the language in recent years did not seem to matter. She went on Matt Lauer's *Today Show* to try to counter the accusations, but to her chagrin it worsened her situation because she appeared to be able to cry without shedding any tears. Some in the media referred to her performance as a "13-minute mea culpa." Moreover, everything back-fired as her defensive strategy was seen as suspicious and untruthful, and the news media was biased against her from the very beginning. Within a few days, Dean had lost 10 sponsors (Potter 2014).

- Is it fair that Paula Dean was demonized in the media for using the N-word while hip-hop superstars use the N-word routinely and they are celebrated by the same media?
- What do you suppose is the image of black or Hispanic Americans who very frequently use the N-word in public?
- Is it ever okay when white people use the N-word, even if they use it infrequently, and privately?
- Is it a form of racism to accept that it is okay for black or Hispanic people to use the N-word and hold white people to a higher standard?

By using the defensive strategy of an *apology* (also called a concession), the user wants others to see him or her as acting out of character with what happened, though the user agrees that what happened was wrong. In some cases, the person will also offer compensation. Recipients often view such actions as insincere, especially if the user chose to lie about the situation in the first place.

Representative Anthony Weiner's apology strategy illustrates a liar's paradox as explained in the Window into Practical Reality 2.4.

Window into Practical Reality 2.4

Anthony Weiner and the Liar's Paradox

U.S. Representative, Anthony Weiner, from New York discovered that first denying and then apologizing for sending explicit sexual pictures and sexual text messages to women as young as 17 did not make people react favorably toward him. Due to his inappropriate behavior, many of his constituents and fellow representatives asked for his resignation. However, instead of resigning, he resorted to counseling and taking time off from his duties. This corrective attempt fell short, and he eventually was pressured into resigning.

The problem spilled over further into his subsequent bid for the job as New York City mayor. Investigation revealed that the lewd behavior reported earlier continued for an entire year after the original debacle happened, leading to his defeat in 2013 for the mayor's job. To some, Anthony Weiner will always be a liar—not to be trusted. What, if anything, could Weiner have done following the first incident of sexting to restore the trust and confidence of voters?

Accounts include questionable actions or situations based upon the report of a particular person. The believability of such accounts depends upon the credibility of the account giver and the perceived degree to which the content of the account is true. The most important components are the content and the story being told, depending upon the circumstances. The more truthful, reasonable, and normal people are perceived to be, the more likely their content quality will be seen as positive; however, the less truthful, reasonable, and normal the individuals, the more likely their content quality will be interpreted negatively.

Managers' views are shaped by experience, norms, and social protocol in a given situation. If a chosen strategy conflicts or deviates from the manager's view, the effectiveness of the strategy will be diminished. Strategies must be selected based on audience and the context of the situation.

Nonverbal Impression Management

People clearly develop impressions of others from the nonverbal cues they perceive. Despite advancing technology, many cultures in the world still prefer to develop face-to-face business relationships rather than relying on electronic solutions. When you are face-to-face with someone for the first time, within one-tenth of a second the other person is judging your attractiveness, likability, trustworthiness, competence, and aggressiveness, among other things. Technology can facilitate similar connections among individuals. For example, videoconferencing can allow a similar judgment to be made about attractiveness, likability, and other characteristics. Because of the constant sizing-up that occurs from first impressions, introductions can be threatening, whether occurring face-to-face or virtually.

You can do many things to ease the fear and discomfort. Having a positive frame of mind is essential. Before an encounter, do something to relax such as taking a few deep breaths. Study the nonverbal elements of the presentation situation. For example, if you are not sure how much space to give the other party, give more than you think is adequate. In the United States, one full arm's length generally works well. The initiation of eye contact is crucial, because maintaining eye contact generally communicates sincerity and honesty. In some cultures, however, the rules for eye contact differ, especially when involving a male and a female or people of different ages. However, eye contact does not mean the same thing as staring which can be interpreted as somewhat offensive even among those who expect strong eye-to-eye contact. Speaking in a low tone of voice and controlling your movements is also important. Always remember, there is only one chance to make a first impression (Reiman 2008).

Self-confidence and empathy are associated with control; therefore, talking and moving less generally makes a better first impression. There are certain postures that may hold meaning for some people but trying to interpret what someone is saying through these positions may not always be reliable. You will need to learn an individual's nonverbals to be sure that you are interpreting unspoken messages correctly. Strong first impressions take place when the message and the nonverbals align, and when they are both believable. In situations where the two do not align or are not believed, our reaction is often that we could not read the person or that there was something unsettling about him or her. Window into Practical Reality 2.5 reveals the consequence of an unintended gesture.

Window into Practical Reality 2.5

The Ambiguity of a Misinterpreted Gesture

An example of a posture that you may have a self-conceived notion about would be crossed arms. Many people believe that if someone crosses his arms that the person has already made up his mind or that he is not listening any longer. However, if the room is cold, perhaps the person is crossing his arms in an attempt to keep warm. Additionally, many people cross their arms simply because they are more comfortable that way. Some studies suggest that if you see someone else cross his arms, you are more likely to do so. People often mimic gestures in social interactions.

- What postures and gestures do you use that people may misread?
- With a partner, observe and comment on each other's postures and gestures and how they might be perceived.

Nonverbal impressions are very strong during the job interview process. Both the decision of the interviewer to make a job offer and the decision of the candidate to accept are largely based on the impressions that were formed by the initial interview. The behaviors of both parties will include the use of eye contact, facial expression, posture, interpersonal distance, and body orientation. When the interviewer and candidate hit it off during the interview, a positive connection has occurred between the two people that can carry into future exchanges.

Impressions Conveyed by Dress and Behaviors

It is amazing the amount of money that college students spend on preparation for the GMAT, GRE, or LSAT and how little is spent on preparing to get a job after college. Even when career coaching is offered, very few college students take advantage of it. One firm dismissed a college applicant for wearing flip-flops to the interview, and another applicant was dismissed when he was asked why he wanted to work in the field and he responded, "It beats flipping burgers." While business norms are shifting, being a serious job candidate is still necessary. Appropriate attire and behavior speak volumes about you and influence the impression you make on others.

If you have not recently listened to yourself or observed your mannerisms on video, record and analyze yourself. Is what you are seeing what you thought you were doing? How would you react to you? How do you think others will react? During that first impression are others seeing you as knowledgeable, flexible, enthusiastic, and sincere? Even if grooming is not important to you, it may be to others as a sign of your professionalism as well as attention to detail. If you want others to feel confident in your abilities, you must establish eye contact while shaking hands. A posture that is animated but relaxed will appear inviting to the other person. If the position requires authoritative dress, then you need to dress the part.

In one study, subjects were video recorded, and the recordings were assessed by trained decoders for likeability, effectiveness in speaking, expressivity, and confidence. Male subjects who were nonverbally skilled and extroverted and displayed outwardly focused and fluid, expressive behaviors were more favorably received than were those lacking those characteristics. Females who displayed more facial expressiveness made better impressions. A conclusion of the research is that behaviors that make a favorable impression can differ for males and females (Riggio and Friedman 1986).

Impressions Conveyed by the Office Environment

Office design is a form of object language. Personality revealed in the way one arranges and accessorizes his or her office can say a lot to others implicitly. People may initially decide if you are extroverted, conscientious, and open just by looking at your office. A desk against the wall forms a more open arrangement, and the occupant is seen as friendlier and more extroverted then those offices with a closed-desk arrangement. One study looked at the effect of wood furniture and wood floors and found that people perceive offices with wood floors and wood desks and furniture to be warmer and the people who occupy them to be more successful (Ridoutt, Ball, and Killerby 2002).

Research has also indicated that observers' perceptions of office holders whose stacks are organized were more favorable than those with very messy or very clean offices. A recent study found that the portability of the technology the office holder has contributes to the office holder being seen as more extroverted and open to new possibilities (Scheibe, McElroy, and Morrow 2009). Customers also base their image of a company not only on how employees treat them but on their perceptions of the employee's appearance and behavior. For example, Best Buy has their Geek Squad members drive a cute Volkswagen Bug when visiting clients.

Using Your Impressions to Manage Others

Now that we have covered the nuances of impression management, let's examine how you can use these nuances to influence the impressions others will have of you. *Self-monitoring* is being able to control your own cues and read the cues of others. Some researchers consider this part of an individual's personality. Males and females are frequently taught that certain expressive behaviors are okay for one gender but not for the other. Research has also shown that in initial interactions, physically attractive people are judged more favorably than those seen as less attractive.

During negotiation situations, if you make a favorable impression and are seen as cooperative, you maintain your ability to use that impression to influence the other negotiators. However, if during the negotiations you change from cooperative to competitive, the others' impression of you may become increasingly negative. The impression of the other negotiator changes less, though, when they start with a positive impression of you.

Managers must be able to identify honest and manipulative impression management strategies and determine their appropriate use. Organizations and managers must work together to reduce and discourage undesirable strategies, and employees must be conscious of the images they are projecting and understand the audience as well as the situation. It is easy for managers to have a deluded view of their own leadership abilities (self-deception). When in a leadership position, a manager often will exaggerate personal strengths and deny common faults in order to project a positive self-image. The more their employees buy into the manager's position, the more they will believe that their manager is a good leader. In order to be viewed as a positive leader, the leader must impress employees with promises and actions that are seen as successful by the employees. Therefore, managers strive to use a combination of impression management and interpretation of follower expectations to become charismatic leaders.

Managers in every organization reflect and influence the corporate culture on a daily basis. They cannot just use e-mail and texts to communicate values but must interact and have a physical presence with their employees. While internal publications and electronic communications can effectively distribute information, nothing replaces a charismatic, caring manager in making employees feel important to the company.

Summary

The acts that people perform in their daily lives can be compared to theatrical performances in which actors perform in front of an audience on a hypothetical stage. The acting is designed to elicit a desired positive self-image. When not in public view, people can get rid of their personas and be themselves. Impressions are made and solidified continually, either on purpose or by accident. Some people try to direct how others perceive them by using impression management. Impression management involves various elements, including verbal and nonverbal effects, dress and behavior, personal environments, physical appearance, and social roles. Assertive impression management strategies include ingratiation, self-promotion, exemplification, supplication, and intimidation. Defensive impression management strategies include innocence, excuses, accounts, justifications, and apologies.

Your verbal and nonverbal behaviors lead people to decide if you are being truthful or untruthful, sincere or manipulative. Eye contact and posture carry strong messages about your motives and intents, though cultural expectations differ about these elements. Male and female behaviors and expectations for dress are often viewed differently, and members of a society have preconceived notions of how each gender should interact and communicate in the work environment. Office environments and other work environment details impress people either negatively or positively. People make judgments about their superiors based on such nonverbal characteristics, and customers judge organizations on such factors as well. Managing the impressions you make on others can help you to successfully impress your superiors and subordinates, and influence your firm's clients and customers.

CHAPTER 3

Employment Communication

Objectives

After reading this chapter, you will be able to:

1. describe the steps needed in hiring the correct people;
2. explain the five aspects of communication in the personnel selection process;
3. write a post-interview job offer letter and a post-interview rejection letter;
4. discuss motivation theories that can be used as communication tools;
5. explain why managerial reprimand should be used as a teaching tool;
6. conduct proper layoffs and firings.

Introduction

Although we call the people working in business organizations human resources, people are unlike the other resources used in the production function: material, financial, or informational. Employees can, and sometimes do, hold grudges, engage in political sabotage, idle down, do the bare minimum just to keep their jobs, and question your authority when aggravated. People can do a host of other things at work that are hard to detect and that can be devastatingly harmful to productivity. The Window into Practical Reality 3.1 is a historic depiction of how early American workers used the power of subterfuge to unify others in restricting labor output. Many early twentieth-century workers were hostile toward scientific management because of what they perceived to be a threat to their job security.

Window into Practical Reality 3.1

Soldiering: How Taylor Used the Piecework Incentive to Improve Worker Morale

Most people who have studied business have heard about Frederick W. Taylor's book *Principles of Scientific Management.* According to Gabor (2000), Taylor was both revered and despised by workers at Bethlehem Steel in the early 1900s for fear that his methods would create efficiencies that would result in the reduced need for workers.

Taylor observed that soldiering, or loafing, by workers was being used as a passive communication strategy to express dissatisfaction with work standards determined through scientific management calculations. The slowdown effort occurred at both the individual and the systematic levels, resulting in lowered productivity for the entire unit (Taylor 1998). In examining the soldiering that occurred from the business communication perspective, three observations were apparent:

- Workers shared their fears with one another that producing more output would result in less work for fewer workers.
- Workers shared their fears with one another that the pay structure was not directly linked to the work they actually did, thus, management did not know how to systematically link incentives to a worker's productivity.
- Workers shared their views with each other concerning their lack of confidence that the rewards for increased productivity would be equally distributed throughout the workforce.

Workers had little trust for the management, even when the management's perspective was predicated on the assumption that increased demand of goods would be a direct result of the efficiencies proposed by Taylor's designs. In response to the soldiering that was occurring, Taylor instituted a piecework incentive system to encourage increased individual effort, which was facilitated by a production scheduling calendar (Gantt chart) developed by his assistant, Henry L. Gantt. Worker morale improved as a result of scientific management. Taylor's methods resulted in changes in business processes that are still practiced today. For instance, modern food preparation techniques used at McDonald's restaurants and other fast-food operations are based on Taylor's efficiency principles (Bell and Martin 2012).

- Discuss how today's threats of robotics taking away jobs and jobs being shipped overseas are affecting the workers?
- How are workers impacted by reduction in perks such as health care, vacations, and pensions? What if, as some say, there will be no work for humans?

Human resource activities pose various challenges for managers. First, you will need to know how to communicate in a legally compliant way during personnel selection. Second, you will need to know how to select suitable candidates from a sufficiently large pool of applicants, and then communicate and coordinate with others to actually hire the person selected. Third, you will need to know how to write effective offer and rejection messages. Fourth, when you have actually hired a person, you will need to know how to motivate the person you hired to perform well consistently. Finally, you will need to know how to conduct layoffs and firings appropriately.

People are the most important managerial resource, and the most complicated to manage because people are living, breathing entities who harbor a slew of emotions—which can be positive or negative. Using employment communication and improving human resource in your organization is your responsibility.

Improving Human Capital

Human flight, moon landings, submarine missions to the bottom of the ocean, or drilling for oil 5,000 ft below sea level would not have been possible without fully developed human capital. Peter Drucker (1954) said that enlarging human resources permits profit-seeking enterprises to prosper. Human resource is the only resource that is capable of being improved because people can grow intellectually and be developed into managers (Drucker 1954). Despite Drucker's optimism, today's human resources are more difficult to manage than any of the other resources. Managing human resources is—and always will be—predicated on two-way communications and relationship building. The manager's job is to use good communication to improve on human capital by making people more productive. Incidentally, Drucker (1974) appears to be the first business philosopher to use the phrase "managerial communication."

Successful employment communication begins when a manager has grasped the elements of employment communication responsibility. Thus, hiring and retaining excellent people is paramount in improving human capital.

Hiring the Right People

Hiring a new person involves four aspects (1) adhering to equal employment opportunity laws, (2) being familiar with essential and preferred job qualifications for the posted position, (3) conducting productive and legal interviews, and (4) writing effective job offers and rejection messages.

Equal Employment Opportunity Laws

Before any of the aspects of personnel selection can happen, you need to be aware of the equal employment opportunity laws enforced by the federal government, which is essential knowledge for crafting the job description and conducting the interview. Knowledge of the equal employment opportunity law is required to protect the organization against complaints and litigation about discrimination. In the United States, the organization responsible for investigating and enforcing these laws is the Equal Employment Opportunity Commission (EEOC). This government body has a broad range of authority and can investigate complaints against employers brought against them by former or current employees. The equal employment opportunity laws enforced by the EEOC are shown in Figure 3.1.

Title VII of the Civil Rights Act of 1964
This U.S. law makes it illegal to discriminate against someone on the basis of race, color, religion, national origin, or sex. The law also makes it illegal to retaliate against a person because the person complained about discrimination, filed a charge of discrimination, or participated in an employment discrimination investigation or lawsuit. The law also requires that employers reasonably accommodate applicants' and employees' sincerely held religious practices, unless doing so would impose an undue hardship on the operation of the employer's business.

The Pregnancy Discrimination Act of 1978 (PDA)
This law amended Title VII to make it illegal to discriminate against a woman because of pregnancy, childbirth, or a medical condition related to pregnancy or childbirth. The law also makes it illegal to retaliate against a person because the person complained about discrimination, filed a charge of discrimination, or participated in an employment discrimination investigation or lawsuit.

The Equal Pay Act of 1963 (EPA)
This law makes it illegal to pay different wages to men and women, if they perform equal work in the same workplace. The law also makes it illegal to retaliate against a person because the person complained about discrimination, filed a charge of discrimination, or participated in an employment discrimination investigation or lawsuit.

The Age Discrimination in Employment Act of 1967 (ADEA)
This law protects people who are 40 or older from discrimination because of age. The law also makes it illegal to retaliate against a person because the person complained about discrimination, filed a charge of discrimination, or participated in an employment discrimination investigation or lawsuit.

Title I of the Americans with Disabilities Act of 1990 (ADA)
This law makes it illegal to discriminate against a qualified person with a disability in the private sector and in state and local governments. The law also makes it illegal to retaliate against a person because the person complained about discrimination, filed a charge of discrimination, or participated in an employment discrimination investigation or lawsuit. The law also requires that employers reasonably accommodate the known physical or mental limitations of an otherwise qualified individual with a disability who is an applicant or employee, unless doing so would impose an undue hardship on the operation of the employer's business.

Sections 102 and 103 of the Civil Rights Act of 1991
Among other things, this law amends Title VII and the ADA to permit jury trials and compensatory and punitive damage awards in intentional discrimination cases.

Sections 501 and 505 of the Rehabilitation Act of 1973
This law makes it illegal to discriminate against a qualified person with a disability in the federal government. The law also makes it illegal to retaliate against a person because the person complained about discrimination, filed a charge of discrimination, or participated in an employment discrimination investigation or lawsuit. The law also requires that employers reasonably accommodate the known physical or mental limitations of an otherwise qualified individual with a disability who is an applicant or employee, unless doing so would impose an undue hardship on the operation of the employer's business.

The Genetic Information Nondiscrimination Act of 2008 (GINA)
This law makes it illegal to discriminate against employees or applicants because of genetic information. Genetic information includes information about an individual's genetic tests and the genetic tests of an individual's family members, as well as information about any disease, disorder or condition of an individual's family members (i.e., an individual's family medical history). The law also makes it illegal to retaliate against a person because the person complained about discrimination, filed a charge of discrimination, or participated in an employment discrimination investigation or lawsuit.

Figure 3.1 Equal employment opportunity laws

Source: EEOC (2017).

After the EEOC has investigated a complaint, it can issue the complainant a letter called a Right to Sue Letter. Once issued, in many cases, a former or current employee, who believes that he or she has been the victim of discrimination (when at least one of the laws enforced by the EEOC has been violated), can bring a cause of action against the employer in the appropriate court of jurisdiction. A Right to Sue Letter strengthens the legal arguments for a party or parties bringing forth a cause of action claiming discrimination; nevertheless, these lawsuits can be expensive for both parties and take many years to be resolved.

The EEOC can also file an independent lawsuit against an employer on behalf of workers it deems to have suffered from disparate treatment or disparate impact. According to the EEOC (2018), 84,254 workplace discrimination charges were filed with the federal agency nationwide during fiscal year (FY) 2017, and $398 million were secured for victims in the private sector and state and local government workplaces through voluntary resolutions and litigation. The reputation and image of the accused organization is always hurt when discrimination lawsuits become public knowledge, as illustrated in the Window into Practical Reality 3.2.

Window into Practical Reality 3.2

Walmart in the Courts

Retail giant Walmart gained a lot of negative attention from the facts surrounding a class-action lawsuit filed on behalf of former female employees in 1998. U.S. District Court Judge Martin Jenkins granted a class-action status to 1.6 million current and former female Walmart employees who charged that the company was paying women less and promoting them proportionately less often. Lower court cases had already been heard and decided in favor of the workers. [*Dukes vs. Walmart Stores, Inc.,* No. C01-02252 MJJ (U.S. District Court for the Northern District of California).] The main facts presented to the court as evidence of discrimination were produced by Dr. Richard Drogin, a professor emeritus from California State University, Hayward:

- The hourly rate for female workers was up to 37 cents less than their male counterparts.

- Full-time female employees earned on average of nearly $5,000 less than male employees in yearly salary while working more than 45 hours per week.
- Only 33 percent of managers were female, yet females made up 72 percent of the company's workforce.
- Only 14 percent of Walmart store managers were women, yet women made up 92 percent of the company's cashiers.

The Supreme Court, in June of 2011, reversed the lower court rulings and ruled in favor of Walmart stating that the group of approximately 1.6 million females included in the class-action lawsuit was unmanageable and did not give Walmart a fair opportunity to adjudicate all of the numerous noncohesive claims as they pertain to EEOC laws and the precedent already established by the lower courts. The plaintiffs had failed to establish the glue that held so many separate claims together. Nevertheless, with so many women in Walmart's workforce and customer base, the alleged charges of gender disparity in pay and promotions did not sit well with many and hurt the company's public reputation (Walmart 2011).

Flash forward seven years. CNBC's Lauren Thomas and Courtney Reagan (2018) reported that Walmart did well by its employees. Walmart was among the first of conglomerate retailers to offer a starting hourly wage rate of $11 for employees in the U.S., following the passage of the new tax law in December 2017. Walmart also announced that it would expand maternity and parental leave benefits, and it would pay a one-time bonus to eligible employees (those with 20 or more years of service) of as much as $1,000. Walmart's generosity will cost an estimated $400 million for fiscal year 2018 (Thomas 2018). Walmart's recent gestures of generosity have done a lot for its positive public image and has more than likely weakened any claim that Walmart does not care about its employees, whether male or female.

Job Qualifications

As a hiring manager, you will have to be familiar with the *necessary job qualifications,* a set of skills essential for success in the job, so that you can conduct a productive and legal interview, and eventually hire a qualified applicant. The job description and the job specifications are composed after analyzing a job. The *job description* is the detailed explanation of what a person in that position actually has to do. The *job specifications* are the listings of mental and physical skills and abilities required to perform the job, that is, educational level, certification, training, and so on. When a job opening is posted, it will normally include both the necessary and preferred qualifications.

The interviewing manager should have a written job description that clearly lists the responsibilities of the position. The job description items can also be used when composing the advertisement for the position. Current law requires that hiring managers select only those candidates for interview who possess all the *necessary qualifications* listed in the advertised position pertaining to what the employee will be doing, and their tasks, and responsibilities. This requirement is an effort to make hiring practice more systematic and fair among all employers. Under EEOC guidelines, it is illegal to invite a candidate who does not have all the advertised necessary qualifications for an interview.

The manager should also have knowledge of the *preferred job qualifications*: an optimal set of skills desired by an employer of a job applicant, but not required for an interview. Organizations often utilize search committees, whose job it is to write and place the advertisements, review the applications, invite the candidate in for an interview, and recommend hiring or not hiring the individual. In some instances, the search process is managed in the HR department, while in others the search process is more decentralized and may occur in the department where the opening exists or in conjunction with HR personnel. Current EEOC guidelines do not require managers to select candidates for interview, who possess all or some of the preferred qualifications listed in the advertised position. Nonetheless, a person who possesses all of the necessary qualifications and most of the preferred qualifications would stand a good chance of being interviewed. In fact, a sufficiently large group of candidates should be selected for prescreening for the position based on the stated qualifications, as some typically will be excluded or drop out of the search.

If the applicant has done his or her homework, the person has a resume that made you sit-up and take notice, a cover letter that dazzled you, good manners, and sharp interview skills. In such instances, hunting for the perfect candidate is easy. However, very few candidates will actually make your job of hiring this easy. Currently, 92 percent of recruiters say they are using social media to find the high-quality candidates they desire (Bynum 2017). This means that you as the recruiter will have to search for your candidates; they will not fall into your lap.

Conducting a Legal Interview

As manager, you must compose appropriate interview questions that are legally compliant and conduct effective and legally compliant interviews. Both the interviewer and the interviewee have objectives. The interviewer has three main goals: (1) to collect information—is the applicant qualified to do the job and will the applicant do the job, (2) to provide information—give the candidate a realistic preview of the company and job to entice them to accept the job, and (3) to check the personal chemistry or candidate's fit with the organizational culture. The interviewer can then determine if the candidate is capable of doing the job, and if he or she has a personality that fits the organization. On the flip side, the interviewee has the objectives of (1) presenting information, (2) collecting information, and (3) checking personal chemistry to assess the personalities and styles of people with whom they might be working. Figure 3.2 provides a summary of the proper steps to take in the interview selection process.

It is important that you ask legal questions that adhere to EEOC guidelines. Inexperienced managers can cause their employers much grief and embarrassment by asking illegal and inappropriate interview questions. Figure 3.3 presents some common hiring dilemmas and provides answers and strategies to help you plan and carry out interviews more effectively.

Step 1 **Plan and prepare for the interview.**	1. Assure that interviewers have a firm grasp of the objectives of the interview. 2. Plan the interview around the determined objectives. 3. Study the requirements of the job and the characteristics of an ideal candidate.
Step 2 **Build the interview prior to considering each candidate.**	1. Custom build the interview around the job description. 2. Make sure all relevant topics are covered during the interview. 3. Keep complete files that include supporting documents of *each* candidate.
Step 3 **Be sure the evaluation process is job related.**	1. Carefully evaluate the applicant's credentials given the job's requirements. 2. Make a proper determination of the applicant's willingness and fit. 3. Take notes during the interview to assist in later deliberation.
Step 4 **Make sure all interviewers abide by EEOC guidelines.**	1. Be sure to consult with legal counsel if you have doubt about the legality of a question. 2. Be sure each question has a job-related purpose. 3. Be sure that your selection decision is and properly documented.

Figure 3.2 Steps in the selection interview

Situation	Response
Situation 1. George is a history professor who struggles to speak Spanish as a second language. He is working on a book, subsidized by the university where he has tenure, about a particularly old border town in Texas near the Mexico border. He wants to hire an assistant to help him when he interviews local residents who have lived in the area for more than 45 years. Because many of these older residents speak only Spanish, George asks applicants routinely, "Do you speak Spanish?" Is this an appropriately legal interview question? Which law in Figure 3.1 might or might not be violated?	**Answer 1.** If the individual needs to be able to speak Spanish to do the job, then that should be a requirement in the job postings for the position. This is called a bona fide occupational qualification. Title VII of the Civil Rights Act of 1964 is applicable.

Figure 3.3 Employment process dilemmas and suggested strategies

Situation	Response
Situation 2. Simon is interviewing Mary for an administrative assistant position. Mary's cell phone rings and she answers the call during the interview. Mary's face changes from smiling to a cautioned shocked look. From the tone of the conversation, Simon can pick out bits and pieces from what the other person is saying to Mary. Simon infers that a boyfriend has just broken off a relationship with Mary. Simon wonders what this could lead to, if Mary is hired. She is also thick around her waist area and appears pregnant. Would it be appropriate for Simon to try to find out more about Mary's crisis? What law in Figure 3.1 governs this situation between Mary and Simon?	**Answer 2.** It would be illegal for Simon to ask Mary any personal questions about the call and whether she is pregnant. The PDA of the EEOC law covers this. Mary also should have had her phone turned off and never taken the call. Her tendency to take personal calls during an interview would likely be viewed negatively as an indication of how she would behave on the job.
Situation 3. Jennifer has completed the application and review processes for hiring for an outside sales position and is now interviewing candidates. She clearly states, as a part of the interviewing process, that the candidates must be able to load and unload a truck with boxes weighing approximately 30 pounds each at least twice each day. Therefore, she asks each candidate, "Will you need a reasonable accommodation to do the job as described?" Is this question a legally appropriate question? Why? What federal law makes it so?	**Answer 3.** The question is appropriate. The lifting requirement can be considered a bona fide occupational requirement at the time of hire. However, if the health status of the individual changes after being hired in the position, the company may have to make reasonable accommodations. However, this does not mean that you must reduce the standards to accommodate the person who has a documented legal disability. Title I of the ADA of 1990 is applicable.
Situation 4. Jim has completed interviews with three candidates for a sales representative position. One interviewee, Fred, was very boastful of his sales performance at a previous job. Jim's curiosity was aroused during the interview, so he called the previous employer and spoke with Fred's former direct supervisor to get more clarification on Fred's job performance. Was Jim within his legal rights to seek and confirm information about Fred's job performance with a previous employer?	**Answer 4.** It is against the law to call a current employer without the applicant's consent, as you might endanger the person's livelihood. However, if he listed the current supervisor as a reference, you may call that person. You may call any former employer for whom the applicant is no longer working.

Figure 3.3 (Continued)

Impression Management

Impression management is frequently used during interviews as self-focused and others-focused tactics. Self-focused tactics include exemplification, internal attributions, intimidation, professionalism, self-promotion, and supplication. Others-focused tactics include bargaining, favor rendering, appealing to higher authority, opinion conformity, other enhancement, ingratiation, and supervisor-focused tactics (Peck and Lavashina 2017). The interviewers must ask sufficient questions to be sure that the person can do what they say they can and that they fit the company's needs.

Correspondence with Candidates

Once a decision has been reached as to whom to hire, the manager or his designated person would then write a job offer message or a rejection message to each candidate. An example of an effective offer message and an effective rejection message are presented in Figures 3.4 and 3.5.

Ms. Jane Smith
62 Sessions Avenue
St. Louis, MO 63111

Dear Ms. Smith:

Thank you for coming in and interviewing with our search team on January 13, 20—.

We would like to offer you a position as an entry-level sales associate. Should you accept, your start date will be Monday, February 20, 20—, with a salary of $45,000, plus sales bonuses. You are also eligible to receive health insurance and have the option to participate in a 401(K) plan. The benefit programs will be described to you more fully on your first day on the job. Please plan to report to work at 8:30 a.m. for your orientation and initial training.

Please respond with your acceptance of the job offer by January 20, 20— . If we do not hear from you by that date, we will assume you are not interested in the position. If you have any questions about the position, please call me at 901-222-9103. We are looking forward to having you join our team.

Sincerely,

Maxine Patterson
Maxine Patterson
Sales Director

Figure 3.4 The post-interview offer letter

Ms. Jane Smith
62 Sessions Avenue
St. Louis, MO 63111

Dear Ms. Smith:

Thank you for taking the time to come in and interview with us on January 13, 20—. We have finished the interviewing process for the entry-level sales position and have found another candidate whose qualifications more closely match the requirements of the job.

While we have only one position to fill at this time, please feel free to apply again when other positions become available.

Sincerely,

Maxine Patterson
Maxine Patterson
Sales Director

Figure 3.5 The post-interview rejection letter

It is important that all interviewees receive a communication from the firm as quickly as possible after the interview. Send the offer letter before you send the rejection letters and wait for a reply from the candidate that you wish to hire. A formal rejection letter should then be sent to all applicants who applied but did not get the job. While you are waiting on the response to your job offer, you may want to go ahead with sending rejection messages to those candidates whom you are certain you will not be hiring.

Motivating Human Capital

Many of the best theories in management come from applications of sociology and psychology in the management environment. Even though these fields of study have a foundation in reinforcement theory and other aspects of personal and social behavior, their business application is impossible without using good communication. No matter how a manager might view theories of motivation, keeping employees motivated means that managers will need to observe and talk to their employees to find out what types of rewards and punishments make them tick! Three theories have immediate employment communication applicability: (1) equity theory, (2) expectancy theory, and (3) the formal reprimand.

Equity Theory

An important part of a manager's job is always to be aware of the feelings of inequity in pay or responsibilities among workers. These feelings of inequity often lead to loafing, employees doing the minimum just to keep their jobs, or high levels of unexplained turnover—meaning employees' leaving their jobs for no apparent reason. Frustrated workers may at times abuse customers and clients as well as their fellow workers. Adams's (1963) *Equity Theory* is predicated on three assumptions applicable to most employment communication situations:

- The equity norm is a social assumption that an employee will expect a fair return for the contribution they make to the job.
- The social comparison is a determination that employees make as to whether their returns for the work they do is equitable in comparison to others' inputs and outcomes.
- When employees feel their equity is less than others' equity, they will seek to reduce the inequity in three ways: (1) cognitively distorting inputs and outcomes known as cognitive distortion, (2) altering their inputs and outputs, and (3) quitting the organization. (Bell and Martin 2012)

External pay equity can be assessed by comparing your employees' salaries with industry averages for pay standards. Manpower.com publishes an *Annual Salary Guide* free to the public available online that includes approximately 200 job titles. The United States Department of Labor, Bureau of Labor Statistics, publishes an annual reference book, available for free online, entitled the *Occupational Outlook Handbook* that includes several hundred job titles with industry outlooks, earnings, and educational requirements. Also, be sure that every employee is regularly evaluated and rewarded for good work. Remember that perceptions of fairness and equity are always a two-way employment communication responsibility.

Expectancy Theory

Expectancy theory is a motivational model that seeks to explain or predict task-related effort. It assumes the making of conscious choices among alternatives. The theory suggests that motivation is determined by two individual beliefs that (1) effort and performance have a relationship, and (2) desirable work outcomes are associated with differing performance levels (Vroom 1964). Motivation is then viewed as a function of the perceived relationship between an individual's effort, his or her performance, and the desired consequence of the outcomes of performance. The key terms to understanding the model are *expectancy*—a belief that effort is followed by performance; *instrumentality*—a mental calculation that an achieved task performed will lead to a work outcome; and *valence*—the value the individual places on the outcome.

Experienced managers know that the best application of this theory is in the recognition that all expectations can be shaped through good, honest communication. As a manager, do not create faulty expectations or make implied promises. Do as you say you will do. Evaluate your employees fairly. You can understand what your employees expect and value only by talking honestly with them about what they want versus what you can realistically deliver, when they perform as they said they would.

Reprimanding to Motivate

A *formal written reprimand* is an aversive control that can include both negative and positive reinforcements to correct undesirable employee behaviors. Reprimands deter employees from engaging in workplace behaviors that could pose a hazard to a company's profitability in future. The ideal reprimand should stamp out unproductive workplace behaviors and endorse productive behaviors shown in detail in Figure 3.6 (Bell and Ramdass 2010).

The model shown in Figure 3.6 is a depiction of the managerial reprimanding process. In this model, managers are depicted as keen observers, judging whether employees' behaviors are productive or unproductive, and then rewarding or punishing accordingly. Managerial reprimand in the workplace is the means by which supervisory personnel correct behavioral inadequacies and ensure adherence to established company policies. Moreover, a positive approach may resolve behavioral problems without having to reprimand. However, if unacceptable behavior is a persistent problem or if the employee is involved in a misconduct that cannot be

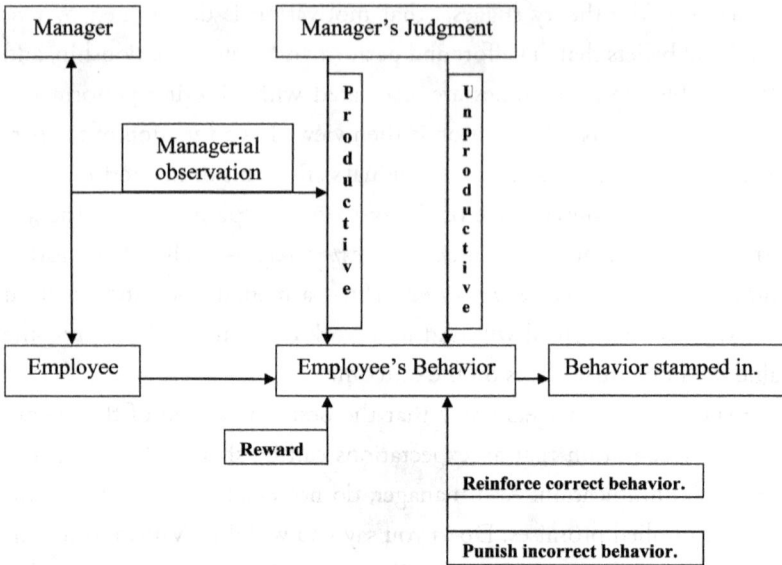

Figure 3.6 The managerial reprimand model

Source: Bell and Ramdass (2010, p. 4).

tolerated, managerial reprimand should be used to correct the behavior. More importantly, managerial reprimand should not be used to embarrass an employee.

The managerial reprimand model can be explained as a three-step process

- Employee Behavior—first, the employee behavior is displayed in the workplace.
- Manager's Observation—second, is the employee's behavior as objectively observed from the manager's perception acceptable or unacceptable?
- Behavior Reinforcement—third, if acceptable, action is taken to reinforce good behavior. If unacceptable, action can be taken to identify the unproductive behavior or policy violation, and punishment imposed if needed.

An effectively written reprimand can also be a useful teaching tool. The manager's goal is to write a three-paragraph reprimand that will help modify the rule-breaker's behavior, while at the same time avoiding hostility, enmity, and other forms of emotional baggages normally associated with poorly constructed and administered reprimands. Normally, a tiered system of progressive discipline (verbal warning, first-written warning, second-written warning, and dismissal) is used to punish rule-breaking behavior. For example, an employee's failure to read the shift schedule has resulted in that employee's tardiness—a direct violation of company policy. Let us imagine that the employee's supervisor will reprimand the tardiness infraction. Can the reprimanding supervisor anticipate the employee's answers to the following questions? Can the employee who has just received the reprimand answer the following questions, after the fact?

- How did my actions result in the *incident* leading to my being reprimanded?
- What is the managerial *rationale* for my being reprimanded; in other words, how did my actions pose a hazard to the bottom line (any goal the manager is trying to achieve)?
- Is there accuracy and fairness in the reprimand that I received?
- What is the consequence for my rule breaking and what is the *remedy* for my corrected action?

Once the manager has thought about and answered these four essential questions, the writing process can begin. It can also become a very important legal document for attorneys, if a terminated worker decides to litigate after receiving a Right to Sue Letter from the EEOC (Balloch 2010). Figure 3.7 illustrates the pattern for writing the reprimand which includes three paragraphs: the incident, the rationale, and the remedy.

Having to reprimand an employee, particularly in today's litigious environment, is very difficult for most managers. However, putting everything down in writing and having both people sign it with a human resources representative present generally works very well. Many states have laws that deal with how you must document the infractions of employees who are not performing satisfactorily before you can fire them. While the manager's hope is that the person will cease the actions that led to the reprimand, sometimes it does not, which then leads to a second and third reprimand letter and subsequent discussions before the person

TO: Jack Johnson, employee number 155333

FROM: Jane Doe, Frontline Supervisor

RE: Tardy for a Scheduled Shift

DATE: January 20, 20—

In the first paragraph, describe the incident, such as "On such date, Mr. or Ms. John or Jane Doe did not. . ." Avoid your own emotional spin and keep the content objective. The incident description is merely a summary of the facts: date of occurrence, place, time, persons involved, policy violated, and so on. State all the facts in this paragraph, but, be brief. First-person language (I, me, my) and second-person language (you, your) is acceptable in your final draft reprimand.

Construct the second paragraph to explain management rationale for the write-up and the effect that the incident had on the department or unit or on the bottom line. An example might be, "Jane or John, your behavior resulted in a $3,000 loss in sales due to. . ." Most frontline workers will not be thinking in these terms: often, they do not know how or why their behavior is unproductive. You must use the reprimand as a teaching tool. This is the paragraph to emphasize your rationale to the employee. Most workers should be assumed to be moral; furthermore, when told of the costs of their behavior in terms of profitability or safety or some other goal, most employees will change for the better.

In paragraph three, you will impose a required remedy to correct the behavior. An example might be, "You will notify the immediate supervisor (insert name) in the event you cannot. . ." The document will have a place for the employee and the supervisor or manager to sign. On your first draft, avoid first- and second-person language to keep your own feelings in check. Once you know what you want to say and how to say it, then first- and second-person writing is fine. Use unambiguous language throughout.

Employee,   Supervisor,

Jack Johnson   Jane Doe

Figure 3.7 The three-paragraph reprimand overview

Source: Bell and Martin (2010).

can be legally fired. Figure 3.8 is an example of a well-written reprimand that clearly states the (a) incident, (b) rationale, and (c) remedy.

Layoffs and Firings

Part of a manager's job is layoffs of people when economic times are difficult for a company. In a *layoff,* employees are not allowed to continue working at the present time, but there is an option of reemployment when economic times improve for the company that laid them off. A corporation may have to downsize for a number of reasons including economics, restructuring of the organization, competitive environment, domestic

TO: Jack Johnson, employee number 155333

FROM: Jane Doe, Frontline Supervisor

RE: Tardy for a Scheduled Shift

DATE: January 20, 20—

(a)   On January 3, 20__, our client James Erin with Hadley Enterprises tried to contact the office to obtain information and layouts for an advertisement that was needed that day. Since there was no notification that you would not be at work, the expectation was that you would be covering the office while I was traveling. As you were not in the office, Mr. Erin could not reach anyone, resulting in his inability to get the information he needed for his advertisement, lack of contact with his customers, and loss of potential sales.

(b)   While it is always important to make me aware of when you will not be in the office, it is particularly important when I also am out of the office. Your position requires you to work from 8:00 a.m. until 5:00 p.m., unless other arrangements are made with me in advance. If I am not available by phone or e-mail to make an exception to your work hours, then it is expected that you will be at your desk as the position requires. The position you hold is essential to our customers obtaining critical advertisement materials that help them and us sell products, which in turn pays our salaries. When employees fail to fulfill their responsibilities, there is no income to pay salaries and the company closes.

(c)   In the future, please give me advance notice when you need to change your hours. If the reasons are sufficient, I will do what I can. However, when I am traveling, it is essential that you are at your desk. This is a warning letter concerning this behavior. Now that you understand the importance of your position, it is expected that this will not happen again.

Employee   Supervisor,

Jack Johnson   Jane Doe

Figure 3.8 A three-paragraph reprimand example

Source: Bell and Martin (2010).

or international changes, mergers, acquisitions, or divestitures. Whatever the reason, many times the workers being laid off are good employees and the circumstance causing their layoff is beyond the control of the manager having to communicate the situation.

One of the main considerations during layoffs is how to keep the rest of the employees, who are not being laid off, motivated, as well as telling those who are being laid off why they have been selected. Layoffs are like funerals: you must be clear in your choice of words; you must be sympathetic in your tone; and, above all, consistent in what you say to everyone. It is helpful if the firm has a plan. Some firms hire professional communicators to write, script, and review the messages that are to be directed to people being laid off, as well as other constituents. Of course, the first thing a company will likely do is to eliminate all contract and temporary employees before terminating the permanent ones. Be honest about your company's situation before the layoffs so that the people are not surprised. Keeping employees' loyalty and trust should be of utmost importance to the managers.

It is also necessary for the top management to understand that the managers who lay off people and the employees who survive the layoffs will often have feelings of guilt, fear, anger, distrust, and depression. Survivors will need a great deal of information before, during, and after reductions in the workforce. Top management and managers need to communicate to employees on all levels, which can help to minimize the confusion, panic, and rumors that typically occur during times of layoffs or downsizing. The more that management can reduce the stress through communication, the more the survivors are likely to help keep the organization healthy (Pfeil, Setterberg, and O'Rourke 2003).

Laying off an employee is a very delicate transaction. It is painful for the recipient and should be done by the immediate supervisor, and not by the human resources department. It is also difficult for the manager, however, because many times there is a long-standing friendship involved. Managers who will be doing the layoffs should be coached to be sure that they have the answers they need for the employees. It is important that the employees affected be told about their layoff before other workers or the media are made aware of the situation. After the employees involved in a significant layoff are told, the news media should be made aware of what has happened and why. Many times local, state, and federal government officials also need to be informed. For a publicly traded company, the U.S. Securities and Exchange Commission (SEC) requires that large layoffs be disclosed in writing and submitted to the SEC. Notifying customers and suppliers may also be necessary (Pfeil, Setterberg, and O'Rourke 2003).

Employees should be told of their layoffs face-to-face; it is the only channel that is acceptable. Phone, e-mail, or third-party consultants should never be used. If the company can afford a severance package, it should be offered and explained at the time of the layoff. Generally, the higher the employee is in the organization, and the longer the employee has been employed, the more inclusive the severance package should be. This package tells an individual how much the company truly appreciated his or her work, and says a lot to the employees who remain. Of course, the timing of a layoff can be very important. The day preceding a holiday or the day of return from vacation are not good times to lay off workers. Some companies practice escorting the people laid off out of the building, though this can have negative consequences. Layoffs affect many lives in the organization and can be a tremendous emotional drain on the remaining employees. Try to inform all people being laid off at the same time, rather than dragging out the situation.

As with a crisis response plan and other strategic plans, having a formal layoff plan developed in advance of crisis is good preparation for the rainy day when you have to use it. Once the layoffs are completed, the managers must then cope with the remaining employees to bring stability to the workplace. Survivor's guilt is a real phenomenon that requires appropriate response from management. Open two-way communication is essential to rebuilding and strengthening the credibility of the leadership. Taking a measure of the organizational climate after the event and pinpointing problems and handling them is very important to the future of the firm.

Firing, terminating the employment of a person for a just cause, should always be put in writing. No matter how careful we are in hiring employees, sometimes the arrangement just does not work out. Either the employee is not equipped to handle the position, or the behavior of the employee makes termination necessary.

Firing is unpleasant, which is why you must abide by the appropriate laws and have a fair, consistent policy to follow. It may be a good idea to meet with your corporate attorney or legal counsel in advance of the firing to be sure that all laws are being followed, especially when an illegal behavior has been committed by the employee. Generally, firings are preceded by reprimands. As much as is possible, all reprimands and the firing should be done through face-to-face communications. It is generally a good idea to have someone else present when the firing occurs, such as a human resource's representative or another manager. As with a layoff, your tone of voice should be firm but empathetic, and you should explain the specific reason the firing is taking place, and state the news of the firing unequivocally. The employee should be told when he or she will receive the last paycheck and how you will respond to calls for references. The individual should be allowed to collect personal items, and you will need to collect keys, computers, cell phones, and other corporately owned objects. Following the firing, you may wish to have the individual escorted from the building.

After the employee leaves the office, squelch rumors by informing the staff of the action taken. This can be done by e-mail to speed the delivery and make sure that everyone receives it quickly. Because the details of the separation should remain private due to legal requirements, the statement may simply say that the employee is no longer with the company.

Summary

Human resources are always the most important type of managerial resource and the most complicated to manage. Employees can, and sometimes do, become disgruntled, idle down and do the bare minimum, question managerial authority, and negatively influence colleagues as well as customers and clients. Despite the negatives, when employees are properly motivated through good communication, organizations can achieve remarkable goals. Acquiring human resources requires managers to use communication appropriately in the personnel selection process; the manager's job is to improve human capital, that is, to attract and develop people through effective communication.

The personnel selection process includes (1) knowing about equal employment opportunity laws; (2) identifying essential and preferred qualifications being sought; (3) conducting legal interviews; and (4) writing effective job offer and rejection letters.

The organization responsible for investigating and enforcing equal employment opportunity laws in the United States is the Equal Employment Opportunity Commission (EEOC). Necessary job qualifications are the written job description that clearly lists the responsibilities of the position. Current law requires that all hiring managers select only those candidates who possess all of the necessary qualifications listed in the advertised position. Preferred job qualifications being sought are not required, but they are desired over and above the necessary qualifications.

Inexperienced managers can cause their employers much grief and embarrassment by asking illegal and inappropriate interview questions. Both the interviewer and the interviewee have objectives and goals, and each is trying to determine if a good fit exists. An offer letter will be sent to the candidate selected for the job after the interview. A formal rejection letter should be sent to all the applicants who applied and were interviewed but did not get the job.

Equity theory is predicated on three assumptions applicable to most employment communication situations: equity norms, social comparison, and cognitive distortion. *Expectancy theory* suggests that motivation is determined by the two individual beliefs that (1) effort and performance have a relationship, and (2) desirable work outcomes are associated with differing performance levels.

The managerial reprimand is a teaching tool used as an aversive control measure for rule breakers. The managerial reprimand model represents a process in which managers' use rewards and punishments to mold employees' behaviors toward goals. It has three parts: incident, rationale, and remedy. While the manager's hope is that the person will cease the actions that have led to the reprimand, sometimes it does not, leading to a second and third reprimand letter and discussion before the person can be legally fired, known as progressive discipline. Properly written reprimands should stamp out unproductive behaviors in employees.

Layoffs and firing of people present a very delicate challenge. Layoffs are difficult because good people must often be let go due to adverse situations. Firing is unpleasant, which is why you follow the laws and have as fair and consistent a policy as is possible. Firings should always be put in writing. Once layoffs or firings have occurred, management must communicate effectively with remaining employees to maintain stability in the workplace.

CHAPTER 4

Change Communication

Objectives

After reading this chapter, you will be able to:

1. define change communication;
2. explain change communication strategy in the management functions;
3. discuss how receptivity to change is possible;
4. dislodge ingrained behaviors in yourself and others so change is possible;
5. lead a change communication process;
6. explain the demands, perceptions, and expectations of change communication.

Introduction

Imagine that you have purchased automobile insurance from a leading company for the last 10 years. Another agent from a competing firm approaches you with an offer that he or she says covers a much broader range of damages than your existing policy—and at half the cost because you are married, and have no speeding tickets or accidents in 10 years! Nevertheless, loyalty to your old company and the agent whom you have worked with for many years makes it very difficult for you to switch companies. Six months after you decide not to switch insurers, you have a collision with another vehicle. Your existing insurance company covers only half the damage to your car and the other driver's car. Now the other driver is threatening you with a lawsuit because you received a ticket (violation) from the officer on the scene. Moreover, the person you hit also has an inferior policy and his bodily injury claims are not completely covered by his own insurer. You call the agent from the competing company who offered to insure you, just for clarification purposes. The agent tells you that under the policy he offered, you would have been fully covered regardless of who was at fault. How would you feel about your decision not to change your insurance policy after such an experience? Would you change companies for your future insurance needs? This hypothetical example illustrates, perhaps in an exaggerated manner, the tendency of people to resist change and how the lack of receptivity to change can bring harm to those people and possibly others.

The difficulty of changing an entire organization largely resides in individuals' experiences with changing agendas. When confronted with altering from a comfortable habit to a state in which they have no experience, most people have difficulty saying that yes the change is necessary. For the individual, the change can be something as mundane as selecting a new item on the menu as a substitute for a favorite item that the person has been enjoying for 5 years. Will the change be better than the status quo? *Change communication* is a dynamic, deliberate process that managers use to shift the entire organization from one state of existence to a more desired state of existence, thus affecting every stakeholder of the organization. The change process can be difficult because employees know that change makes demands, and they cannot be sure of what the end result will be. They only know what they have already experienced, and those situations frame their attitudes about change. Employees typically expect to receive something in return for complying with demands placed upon them by agents of change.

Change for an organization is difficult for many of the same reasons that personal change is challenging. Nevertheless, change and the effective communication of it to constituents are essential for an organization's survival. In a recent study of 300 U. S. managers, 65 percent said that communicating clearly and frequently was the most important factor in leading a company or team through a major change (Lipmam 2016; Wolper 2016).

Four aspects of change communication will be discussed: (1) applying change communication strategy in the four management functions; (2) understanding the demands, perceptions, and expectations of change communication; (3) leading the change communication process; and (4) dislodging ingrained practices so receptivity of organizational members to change is possible. We begin our discussion with change communication strategy.

Change Communication Strategy

Barrett (2002) demonstrated that during organizational change, communication with employees can mean the success or failure of the organizational initiative. The input and output mechanisms (open systems theory assumes organizations are dependent on their environments to transform inputs into outputs—goods and service to be sold) happen regardless of whether change comes from a process improvement approach, acquisition, new venture, or merger. Barrett's (2002) model is an attempt to synthesize organizational information into communication.

Figure 4.1 illustrates the application of Barrett's original three-phased change communication model. Figure 4.1 shows both feed-forward loops and feedback loops. Feed-forward represents communications that take place before the fact (encoding and initiating at every level). Feedback refers to communications taking place after the fact (decoding and interpreting at every level). These loops connect each phase of the change

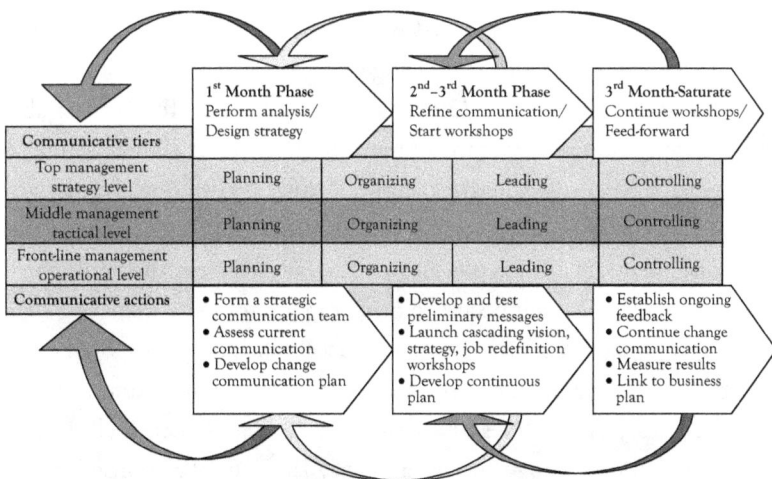

Figure 4.1 The managerial functions and the three-phased communication strategy plan

communication effort back to managers at each organizational level and across the functional areas, thus enabling managers to constantly refine their efforts at shaping employee communications.

Application of the model depicted in Figure 4.1 can help you as a manager achieve your strategic goals in effectively using employee communication to implement change. In high-performing companies, *goals* are usually statements of particular points to be achieved in the short term or long term. Goals tend to be statements of what we want. *Plans* are blueprints for actions needed to achieve the stated goals.

Strategic planning and goal setting serve to (1) illustrate effective employee communications in the context of the high-performing organization; (2) provide a tool to analyze and diagnose a company's communication strengths and weaknesses; and (3) frame the change program to improve employee communications to help drive the change. The three-phase model functions as an analytical tool that helps managers diagnose a company's strengths and weaknesses in employee communication so the company can effectively use communication to facilitate the overall change process.

Receptivity to Change

A well-implemented change strategy requires that stakeholders are receptive to the change, though not every employee will necessarily be supportive. When an organization is involved with continuous change implementation, stakeholders may develop change fatigue or change resistance. Researchers Frahm and Brown (2007) spent 100 days at Tech D, a public sector organization, where many of the employees felt that there were limited feedback channels, and that communication flowed downwards, with little concern about information flow upwards. The research was a case study, and therefore limited to a single firm. Nevertheless, the findings can shed light on change as it occurs in other organizations as well.

Receptivity to change is a measure of acceptance of change by the person, group, or organization. Change receptivity can range from negative, to neutral, to positive. Negative responses to change can include contempt, frustration, change fatigue, and fear. The neutral response includes passive acceptance, limited change readiness, and ambivalence. Positive responses include pro-innovation, change commitment, and excitement.

The receptivity of individuals often changes during the process of the change, which can be for the better or worse. Recognizing that the formal communication was breaking down at Tech D, people began focusing on rumors and grapevine information which, of course, affected productivity negatively. Tech D employees were very satisfied with the CEO's personal communication style; however, middle managers tended not to pass on information. The organization culture was affecting the flow of information. Tech D management knew that they needed to shift their cultural values to improve the organizational communication quality. In many cases, they needed to pre-sell change so that the people involved would understand why it is happening. The people who had access to higher levels of reliable informal communication were more accepting of the changes. Another finding of the study was that people preferred the term *continuous improvement* over the term *change*. The word *change* often carries the connotation of *change for change sake, not secure or positive,* and *personnel turnover* (Frahm and Brown 2007).

As was the case at Tech D, rampant rumors are often associated with unsuccessful change communication efforts, and rumors are often the result of management's poor communication strategies (Burlew, Pederson, and Bradley 1994; Smeltzer 1991; Smeltzer and Zener 1992). Additionally, during periods of change some people choose to leave the organization rather than engage in the change (Douglas, Martin, and Krapels 2006). Many times people are not ready for change, or they do not like the new responsibilities that the changes may call for. When managers explain why the change is necessary, even those who preferred maintaining the status quo, were less resistance to the change. Employees can understand that not changing may increase costs and changing can decrease costs. Because the resistance to change decreases with understanding, the manager's role is very important in framing communication about change. Attitudes depend largely on the framing of the statement by managers (McKay, Kuntz, and Naswell 2013; Spears and Parker 2002).

Employees will respond more positively to organizational change when they are satisfied with the management's communication, and cynicism is greatly reduced when the communication is on the employees' own terms. Change agents will have a better chance of achieving effective and successful organizational change when they consider the needs of different organizational groups (Jones et al. 2008). To inspire employees, a manager's language must transform the change into a vision that is consistent, avoid confusion, and gain credibility with employees (Barnett and Tichy 2000). A manager can be a "meaning maker" by emphasizing the vision and not the details. Metaphors can be effective because of their strong emotional appeal (Conger 1991).

To change communication practices within an organization, you as a manager will need to do the following:

- Learn about the people who will be experiencing the change and decide what the triggers are that will make those people trust you and cooperate with the change.
- Describe the change in a broad way and what you see the change achieving.
- Use dialog to help coach changes in cognitive knowledge to develop new knowledge structures.
- Use training and feedback often to develop the new communication skills that you desire.
- Support for the changes by assuring that all organizational systems are aligned. (Suchan 2006)

A change communication model developed by Wiggins (2008) for use in her communication consulting business is illustrated in Figure 4.2.

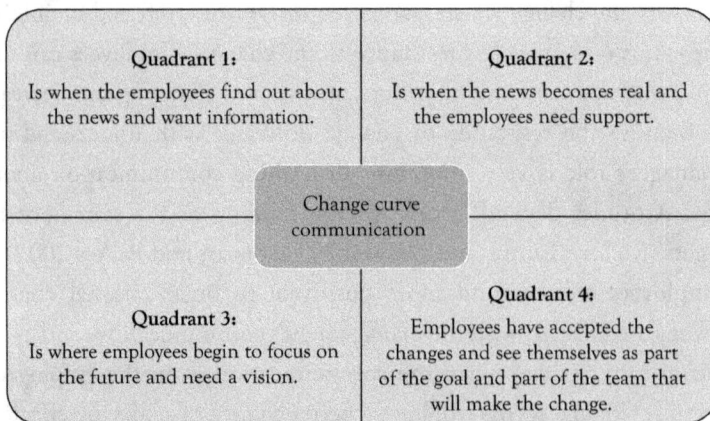

Quadrant 1: Is when the employees find out about the news and want information.	Quadrant 2: Is when the news becomes real and the employees need support.
Change curve communication	
Quadrant 3: Is where employees begin to focus on the future and need a vision.	Quadrant 4: Employees have accepted the changes and see themselves as part of the goal and part of the team that will make the change.

Figure 4.2 *Wiggin's change curve communication quadrants*

As shown in Figure 4.2, employees demand for information changes over time.

- In the first phase (quadrant 1), employees find out about the news and want information. This is the time when holding town hall forums and Q & A sessions at multiple locations using video conferencing would be useful. It is difficult at this time for employees to hear both what management is saying and to listen to their own inner voices with such questions as "Will I lose my job? I have a mortgage!" and so forth.
- In the second phase (quadrant 2), the news becomes real and the employees need support. Management should concentrate on individuals and small groups to make sure that the changes and their impact are understood. Venting is important during this time period, so e-mails to managers, scrawl walls, drawings of bubble people, and texting can help employees relieve stress.
- In the third phase (quadrant 3), employees begin to focus on the future and need a vision. Long-term and short-term goals need to be made with the input of all employees. Management needs to be communicating about the future and employee involvement. Communication interventions should be steady with good information and frequent progress reports, which serve to squelch the rumor mill. Use communication circles to discuss rumors, news stories, and anything else that the employees have heard. Basically, stop the rumor mill.
- In the fourth phase (quadrant 4), employees will ideally have accepted the changes and now see themselves as part of the goal and part of the team that will make the change. Strategies in phase four are unique: management should continue the strategies used in the third phase; however, receptivity and acceptance of the change agenda are assumed in phase four. Managers need to communicate about the future and employee involvement. Communication interventions should be steady with good information and progress reports.

As a manager, you will have to provide employees with a reason to change, and they have to believe that the organization truly wants change.

If employees believe this is merely another fly-by-night idea, they will not give it credence and will not support it.

Dislodging Ingrained Practices

An example of an ingrained practice was a situation in which a governor of Michigan distributed information on a study of the volumes of material in filing cabinets in the various state offices, and the fact that much of the information had not been used for a long time. The governor was concerned because it was much more expensive to maintain office floor space than storage floor space. All offices were instructed to box up old files and send them to the storage facility. One manager was extremely upset with the request and would not take part in determining which materials should be stored. The manager's employees followed the governor's guidelines and emptied six legal filing cabinets from just one department office. The manager did adjust eventually, and of course did not miss any of the materials that were moved. This story illustrates that people require adequate time to adapt to change.

Changing how we communicate is often part of changing a corporation. Altering the way in which workers express their ideas in writing and speaking is challenging at best. Expect questions (and complaints) while change to the new standards is taking place and employees get adjusted to new writing and speaking styles, designs, and message strategies. Standardized communication patterns are important to an organization; however, changing those patterns take time. The more overlap there is between the new communication structures and the old, the easier it will be to make the change.

Cognitive underpinnings for communication strategies that are too simplistic can lead to dysfunctional communication practices and habits, such as documents that are not reader focused in style, organization, or tone; lack of appropriate media (channel) choice; communication distortion caused by too many organizational layers; and not knowing the appropriate feedback channel.

Changes in cognitive underpinnings, organizational performance, and professional self-worth may be necessary to get the message across. Items that can cause inertia in changing the communication in the organization include past and current successes, plentiful resources, systems and structures that are so intertwined that it is difficult to focus, inefficient external feedback loops, and negative information from customers and external stakeholders that may be ignored (Suchan 2006).

Demands, Perceptions, and Expectations

Communication makes demands and creates expectations because communication and information are different: and while they are largely different, the two are interdependent. Information and communication differ in that information is logic and communication is perception. Information is formal, has no shared meaning, and is impersonal. On the other hand, communication is interpersonal. Information becomes communication when there is shared meaning, thus, giving shared experiences primacy over logic (Drucker 1974). According to Peter Drucker, managers must talk to recipients in their own language or on their own terms; that is, one has to use a carpenter's metaphors when talking to carpenters.

Managers leading the change process need to understand that effective managerial communication is associated with less cynicism, fewer harsh feelings, and fewer negative employee perceptions. Direct supervisors have historically been the preferred sources of implementation-related and job-relevant information sharing during change; while senior managers have historically provided avenues for strategic information to be shared throughout the organization.

Change Makes Demands

Changing the way that an organization communicates and uses communication to make change is not easy. Organizations such as Blockbuster, Borders Books, and Montgomery Ward were destroyed when change in the competitive environment made demands that they were not prepared to make. A traveling salesman, Aaron Montgomery Ward, started Montgomery Ward in 1872. By 1883, it mailed out a 240-page catalog listing 10,000 items, and by 1929 it had grown to an unheard-of 531 stores. Industry analysts believe that Montgomery Ward "lost its reason for being," in other words, it lost its mission (Tharp 2000). As a result, the catalog pioneer closed its remaining 250 stores in the year 2000, leaving 37,000 employees without jobs. Montgomery Ward failed because it did not change rapidly enough to meet the demands of innovation in the retail industry. They were not able to motivate stakeholders to do something, become something, or believe something different from the status quo. Generally, if changes are necessary, the changes must be organization-wide, making demands of all involved, including external stakeholders. The entire retail industry is currently under pressure to change in response to the trend toward online purchasing. Whether retailers can make appropriate changes will determine if they survive or die.

One recent example of corporate response to rapid changes in online retailing is presented in the Window into Practical Reality 4.1.

Window into Practical Reality 4.1

Netflix Destroyed Blockbuster in a Case of Change Makes Demands

The battle between Blockbuster (the industry giant at the time) and Netflix (a niche competitor) is legendary. It is an epic battle that lasted from 2004 to 2010. Ironically, had Blockbuster acquired Netflix in 2000 for the small amount of $50 million, Blockbuster would likely be alive today. A Netflix acquisition would have been a meager sum for Blockbuster, which at the time was bringing in billions of dollars in annual revenues.

Nevertheless, change that makes demands is most dangerous when it comes from outside the organization. In this particular case, the most dangerous threat to Blockbuster was the new entry of a small competitor that had mastered an emerging technology foreign to the industry leader. Netflix had first-mover advantage and was rapidly becoming a household name for television streaming and online video delivery. Customers did not have to drive to a store to rent or return a movie!

Vertical integration is generally preferred when a threat from a small competitor occurs. The established company purchases the competition, learns their innovation, integrates their core competency into the existing core competencies, and remains dominant in the industry. Instead of Blockbuster following this tried and true formula, they scoffed at the opportunity to acquire Netflix which had innovated on movie delivery. This would be much to their chagrin later, when Netflix would become too large and lucrative to acquire.

Blockbuster apparently did not realize that online movies streamed to customers' homes were the future already poised to destroy its outdated business model. Moreover, they failed to understand how abrasive they appeared to existing customers, with all the costly and seemingly silly fees, namely, rewind fees for VHS movies and scratch fees for disks. These practices were an internal threat because with Netflix, customers did not need to rewind a downloaded movie or engage with a frustrated Blockbuster staff member about who actually scratched a disk. The market suddenly offered a favorable alternative to Blockbuster.

Even more so, people readily signed up for the small monthly subscriber fee of $4.99 initially charged by Netflix, which gave them access to hundreds of movies they could enjoy at their leisure, and with superior quality to a VHS tape or disk. In 2010, Netflix "subscribers in the United States and Canada grew to the size of the population of Australia" generating $6 billion in annual sales, compared to Blockbuster's $2.2 billion annual sales. (O'Neill 2011). By 2011, *DISH Network Corporation had acquired Blockbuster Entertainment Inc., and the last Blockbuster stores were closed in 2013* (Shaw 2013).

As the Blockbuster failure illustrates, change truly makes demands.

If you consider the situation with Blockbuster, you can see how efforts to change can be counteracted by inertia. Change involves five stages (1) a trigger that is linked with a strategic intent; (2) framed change within the goals to be achieved; (3) dialog to help employees understand and use the change; (4) training programs with feedback to develop the new communication skills; and (5) organizational systems that are aligned in support of the communication changes (Suchan 2006). Selling individuals on change requires considerable persuasion. That often means meeting one-on-one with those who can help promulgate change, and larger scale meetings with all employees.

Change Is Perception

U.S. airlines were doing relatively well financially prior to government deregulation in 1978. Following deregulation, however, many have gone bankrupt or have been acquired by other airlines. In an attempt to remain solvent, various airlines have changed their operations and practices. For example, many flight attendants are no longer permanent employees but part-time employees, which means fewer benefits and lower pay. One might question the long-term benefit of this change in terms of employee morale and passenger satisfaction.

Other changes by the airlines have directly impacted the delivery of service to passengers. Charging for checked baggage is one such example. Check-in bag charges has encouraged passengers to carry more bags onto crowded planes, thus increasing boarding time and leading to more late takeoffs. Most customers' perceptions based on past experience are that checked bags should be part of the flight price, rather than an add-on expense. Customers' negative reactions and outrage, therefore, should not have been unexpected for airline executives. Many doubt the wisdom of other changes that the airlines have made in recent years—charges for food, carry-on bags, assigned seating, and extra leg room are some examples. Sagging employ morale resulting from low wages and benefits further impacts the faltering satisfaction of customers. As a manager, you will need to consider every employee, customer, and stakeholder when communicating organizational change.

Automakers have also been known to miss the mark on customer perceptions, as described in the Window into Practical Reality 4.2.

Window into Practical Reality 4.2

When Asking for $25 Billion in Handouts, Don't Fly There in Corporate Jets

On November 18, 2008, three automobile manufacturing executives flew to Washington D.C. to beg for relief. Their message fell on deaf ears. Why? The image that their actions invoked was similar to a bum wearing a tuxedo on the corner of Fifth Avenue in New York City while begging for a dollar. Members of Congress and the American people did not appreciate the show of extravagance at the same time when they were begging for money.

CEOs of the big three automakers set off a flurry of criticism when they flew to the nation's capital on three separate, private, luxurious jets to make their case to Congress that the automobile industry was running out of cash and needed $25 billion in taxpayer money to avoid bankruptcy. Had all three CEOs—Rick Wagoner of General Motors, Alan Mulally of Ford, and Robert Nardelli of Chrysler—known that actions form a message and set the tone for the communications that follow, they may have thought twice about "exercising their perks" by flying in separate corporate jets to D.C. Perhaps they might have been able to anticipate what disdain their actions would arouse from Congress and U.S. taxpayers.

ABC reported that "Wagoner flew in GM's $36 million luxury aircraft to tell members of Congress that the company is burning through cash, while asking for $10 to $12 billion for GM alone" (Ross and Rhee 2008). Spending $20,000 on a roundtrip flight to ask for a handout illustrates well that what we do, as well as how we do it communicates powerful information to the observer. Oftentimes, the observer's perceptions mean more than the communicator's actions. In hindsight, the three airline CEOs certainly would not have flown to D.C. in separate jets to beg for relief!

Change Is Expectation

Top–down communication provides subordinates with the information needed for understanding. Upper management initiates the change communication process at all levels. When a union is involved, the company should bring them into the change process early on. If the union does not buy in, the organization will have workers who will not buy into the change. In many cases, unions and their members have good reasons to resist the proposed change. It may mean that the company is replacing jobs with robots or shifting operations overseas. While such cost-savings measures may make sense to the firm, it is hard to convince displaced workers that these are improvements. How is it an improvement if they are losing their positions? Do managers know what the union is expecting to see and hear?

One of the most important skills you can apply as a manager seeking to bring about change is the ability to recognize the uncertainty that your people are experiencing and understand it from their perspective. In times of uncertainty, rumors begin to spread quickly through the grapevine and misinformation abounds. Be sure that all employees are receiving the same message during times of change. Formal and informal communication controls need to be in place to control the rumor mill. Because most rumors start because of a lack of information from management, it is better to provide more information rather than too little. A "no comment" management policy simply spurs the rumor mill to run faster! Another important point to remember is that the more employees are involved in solving the problems associated with the change, the less disenfranchised the employees will feel and the more productive your organization will be. If you do not know what is going to happen, say that and ask if the employees would like to work on a solution. Window into Practical Reality 4.3 illustrates how change communication can build expectations.

Window into Practical Reality 4.3

Garnering Trust at FedEx by Communicating Expectations

FedEx has gone through numerous changes since its inception. One of them has been to become a technologically driven company; another was to change from air freight to an air and truck freight corporation. The technological aspect of the company has grown and serves the organization globally. But as the company changed, the types of employees as well as where they were needed changed. To make room for new employees with the functional talents that were needed, the company allowed existing employees to take early retirement. The first round of retirements did not take into account that the company would lose some employees whose talents were sorely needed. At the time of the second retirement incentive, the company limited the number and types of workers who could take advantage of early retirement.

At another point in FedEx history, the pilots from Flying Tiger, a company FedEx had bought out, wanted to organize with a union because Flying Tiger had been a union company. Fred Smith, CEO, wrote a letter to the pilots that he would make it a truck freight corporation if they went through with their plans. FedEx indeed ships a lot of freight today by truck. One wonders if FedEx would have ever become a trucking company at all if the Flying Tigers had not tried to unionize. When the needs of a company change, the company must think through how to bring about the necessary changes. It is also interesting to note that UPS, which was initially a trucking company, now also uses planes. Competition generally calls for companies in the same industry to respond to the changes made by their competition. What industry changes can you think of that started with one company and led to other companies in the industry following suit?

Change Channel Choices

The type of communication channel chosen by a leader for sharing messages is an important component in the change communication process. Sending an e-mail to all personnel with an attachment may not get the workforce sufficiently motivated. However, selling the line managers on the program and having them present it to their workers may work better in some situations; while, holding a series of small meetings with subsets of the workforce, may be preferred in other cases. Whatever the selected channel, allowing employees to have input as the change develops is essential to their buying into the changes. People will backslide by gradually returning to old habits if leadership falters, or if top talent leaves the organization (Duck 2001).

Four key factors in the change process are (1) duration, (2) integrity, (3) commitment, and (4) effort. *Duration* is the time it will take to implement the change and the frequency of reviews while the process is going on. *Integrity* involves choosing the correct people to carry out the change. *Commitment* is the dedication of top management and employees affected by the change to the enactment of the change. Finally, *effort* refers to the amount of resources and energy that will be required to make the initiative happen effectively.

The role of the CEO in both profit and nonprofit organizations in bringing about the desired change is to determine both the direction and strategy for change. Strategic management is a dynamic process that over time determines the long-term performance of an organization. The concept of hierarchy of goals theorizes that strategic-level goal achievement is dependent upon first achieving the goals at both the operational and tactical levels. CEOs can only implement a strategic change when there is an accompanying alignment of organizational parameters at the system level. System-level parameters include organizational structure, culture, training and development, recruitment and hiring, resource allocation, leadership, information systems, reward systems, coordination mechanisms, and control systems (Edwards 2000).

Managers throughout the organization must talk the talk and walk the walk, if they want the players to make the change. Managers must ensure the congruency of the information broadcasted through the formal channels of the organization and the information distributed through the informal channels. It is important that the management team at all levels spend less time writing e-mails and texting, and spend more time developing relationships with their employees by sharing stories of what is happening in the organization, thus developing trust. Some organizations have actually set aside specified days when employees have to communicate with one another in ways other than by e-mails and text messages.

Bennis and Nanus (1985) argue that leaders shape social architecture (organizational culture) by managing meaning through communication. Architects design things that engineers then build. Using this type of simile, executives can apply their leadership to build different types of organizational culture or social architecture. Universities and engineering firms typically use the *collegial style,* with the dominant emphasis on consensus, peer-group membership, and teamwork. *Personalistic style* emerges when a founder's personality personifies the organization, for example CEO Fred Smith at FedEx. With this style, the locus of decision making is within a given individual. The *formalistic style* is at play in government bureaucracy or other hierarchical organizations that drive decisions through explicit rules and policies. Each of these styles is characterized by elements that define an organization's social architecture.

Being Charismatic

Charisma is a personal characteristic that leaders can use to influence people to embrace their vision and initiatives. Success is built on the capacity to transmit image-compelling ideas to the organizational members via sensory modes. Charismatic leaders induce enthusiasm and commitment in others, build trust, and foster positive emotions through their communication and actions. Suzette Haden Elgin (1980) offers perhaps the best explication of "charisma" and what it means when speakers are "Being Charismatic," in chapter 13 of her book. Charisma, loosely defined is the attraction other people have toward a speaker's personality. Charismatic people have attractive personalities. This attraction is purely perception; being charismatic enables the speaker to arouse passion via the sensory mode (sight, touch, smell, hearing, taste) in others—the speaker's words activate while simultaneously soothing the senses. The words charismatic people use, moreover, fall into three categories: parallelism, unifying metaphors, and culturally loaded vocabularies (Elgin 1980).

Successful leaders know that helping the company's leadership to become better communicators is one of the most valuable legacies organizations can leave. Improving communication skills through training is about developing a natural, human, and authentic style. It is about being able to connect with and interest other people, most notably by being charismatic. Window into Practical Reality 4.4 provides an example of how presidential rhetoric was used to evoke change in a nation.

Window into Practical Reality 4.4

President Reagan Changed America by Being Charismatic

Former U.S. president, Ronald Reagan, provides a fascinating example of rhetorical power. Before his election as president, he was an actor by trade and served as governor of the state of California. His presidency saw the fall of the Berlin Wall, the collapse of communism in former Soviet Union, and the challenge of the Iran hostage situation. Possessing charm and charisma, he was viewed by many as a very effective communicator, who knew how to use empathy to develop strong persuasion. He also knew how to surround himself with talented people, who he trusted to do their jobs.

Were people attracted to President Reagan's personality because of his genuineness or because of his acting talents? Could a less charismatic president accomplish what Reagan accomplished?

Remember that as an engaging leader, you will need to be authentic and honest in your communication. Jargon-filled corporate language does not effectively impact employees, and the most convenient channel is not necessarily the most effective. Dewhurst and Fitzpatrick (2007) state that when communicating for change, you should be able to answer the following questions before you form your message:

- Why am I communicating?
- What my team will think?
- What do I want to say?
- What is the best way to say it?

With your answers determined, you will be ready to say what you need to say in the best way possible. Finally, you will want to ask yourself if your communication was successful.

Summary

Effective managers recognize that the recipients' experiences shape the reality of what they see and hear. If managers are to successfully initiate change, they need to mesh the employee communication change program with the functional areas of planning, organizing, leading, and controlling. Five essential actions for an effective strategic communication change program include (1) forming a strategic communication team (SCT); (2) assessing current communication practices; (3) conducting cascading vision, strategy, and job redefinition workshops; (4) monitoring the results; and (5) tying the change communication strategy into the management functions across the management tiers with feedback and feed-forward.

Successfully leading change can include understanding three styles of social architecture: (1) collegial—universities, engineering firms, (2) personalistic—a founder's personality personifies the organization, and (3) formalistic—explicit rules. Leaders manage meaning through vivid and lively communicative actions, and they talk to recipients in their own language and in their own terms.

Managers leading a change program will need to understand that sufficient managerial communication is associated with less cynicism, harsh feelings, and negative employee perceptions. Direct supervisors are the preferred sources of implementation-related and job-relevant information during change, while senior management provides strategic information.

CHAPTER 5

Crisis Communication

Objectives

After reading this chapter, you will be able to:

1. define crisis communication;
2. have a crisis management plan;
3. identify causes of crises and lessons for managing crises;
4. apply the uses of argument in crises;
5. discuss the dangers of managers talking off the cuff;
6. discuss the implications of management failure to identify public sentiment;
7. explain ways in which managers fail to unify empathy.

Introduction

Crises tend to take the form of disasters; problems with products or services; issues with personnel, political, or social upheavals; or ethical breaches. Regardless of the root cause, the organization must work its way out of the crisis successfully if it is to survive. The terror attack of September 11, 2001, tested companies housed in the New York Twin Towers on their responsiveness to a crisis. Fortunately, many of those companies had crisis management plans.

Crisis by definition is a turning point, with momentum heading toward a debacle. Fink (1986) describes this turning point from a business-oriented point of view. He argues that any *prodromal,* or a pre-cursor situation runs the risk of (1) escalating emotions, (2) drawing

harsh media or government scrutiny, (3) disrupting daily business operations, (4) tarnishing the business's image or the image of its executives,
or (5) causing profits to plummet.

Crisis communication occurs when stakeholders look at the organization in crisis to determine if there are victims, if the crisis was accidental, and if the crisis was preventable (Coombs 2007), and then, at how
the management responds to the crisis variables. When a crisis happens,
people often respond emotionally, on who is responsible for the crisis,
the history of responsible parties, and the reputation of those responsible.
If stakeholders believe that the organization caused the crisis, they will
hold it and its management responsible. If the firm has experienced prior
crises, stakeholders tend to be unsympathetic. If the firm has a good reputation, it may be given more leeway to make things right. Social media
has changed where people get their information from and how quickly information, correct or incorrect, can travel. Organizations must now build
positive social media relationships with their constituents so that if they
do have a crisis, the peoples' sensemaking—how individuals and groups
adjust their thinking based on their knowledge—will be positive and not
negative toward the organization.

Crisis Management Plan

All organizations need a crisis management plan. First, you need a crisis management team. It will be their responsibility to understand and
build relationships with the constituents before a crisis occurs. Second,
they will identify different possible crisis situations. Third, they will
formalize a plan for dealing with the crises. Fourth, they will develop
a communications strategy. Fifth, they will hold simulations of a crisis. And sixth, they will be in charge of updating the plan (Kessel and
Masella 2016).

The core crisis management team may change from one type of crisis
to the next. However, the person heading the team must have strong
leadership skills and the authority to activate both internal and external
resources. After identifying possible crises, an action plan should be developed, along with clarifying the responsibilities of each team member.

The communication strategy is next. It is important that all members of the organization know what they can and cannot say in public, as well as who the spokesperson is. The spokesperson must be able to react quickly to get the correct, accurate information out to everyone using multiple media hosts. Organizations can utilize two-way posts such as Google Alerts, Twitter Search, TweetBeep, Tweet Deck, Hootsuite, and Social Mention. It is recommended that a firm develop a before-the-crisis communication strategy, a during-the-crisis communication strategy, and a post-crisis communication strategy. The importance of simulating a crisis is crucial, as it will tell you if you have the correct people in place to deal with the situation. Engaging in the simulation will also help employees overcome the jitters they might otherwise have when a real crisis happens. The simulation also allows the team to make changes to the plan before a crisis happens. Finally, the crisis management team should review the plan on a regular basis.

Social media greatly influences group sensemaking. We start out with a perspective, viewpoint, or framework, and how we receive new information changes those parameters (Klein, Moon, and Hoffman 2006). People today have access to many more media choices, and the information on social media travels very rapidly. Add to that the fact that most of the platforms have no editor overseeing the content for accuracy, and you can see how not only correct but also incorrect information can travel so quickly. The social media phenomenon has made it essential for organizations to develop a relationship with their different constituent groups and develop their trust. Thus, if there is a crisis, the organization will be the first to be believed rather than the last. It has been shown that a firm's involvement in social media before a crisis can reduce the effect of the inaccuracies that spread during a crisis (Veil, Buehner, and Palenchar 2011).

Crises and Management

Not all crises are created equally. Meyers and Holushas (1986) describe nine types of crises as shown in Figure 5.1, together with nine lessons of managing crises offered by Witt and Morgan (2002).

MEYERS AND HOLUSHA'S (1986) NINE TYPES OF CRISES	WITT AND MORGAN'S (2002) NINE LESSONS FOR MANAGING CRISES
Public perception: Quickly take charge, pinpoint the perception problem, get another opinion, construct your best case; cage your lawyers; communicate, establish a spokesperson, accommodate the media; tell your story, and fix the problem.	Find your roots: Prepare a triage plan based on your knowledge of your organization's values.
Sudden market shift: Quiz your customers, find the problem, and respond.	Market the storm: Early warning systems and effective communication networks should be set up immediately.
Product failure: Adjust production; revise the numbers, fix the problem, and return to normal.	A river's gonna go where a river's gonna go: Assess the consequences of walking away from recurring crises.
Top management succession: Smoke out the hidden agenda, assess your options, shelve the boss, announce the successor, observe and support the successor, and enforce the exit	Reconsider the three pigs: Do not trigger a crisis by the changes you make in projects and priorities.
Cash: Take control of the cash, listen hard, stop the hemorrhaging, find the positive, make a plan, raise new cash, reestablish credibility, improve attitudes, and show a profit.	Twine is stronger than string: Clients, suppliers, partners, and stakeholders hit by the crisis need synergy identifiers.
Industrial relations: Size up the climate, open up dialog, isolate the essentials, construct an offer, resume negotiations, reach agreement, and prepare for the next round.	Treat the heart without losing your head: When things are going wrong, the team should be confident and productive.
Hostile takeover: Repel the attacker, assemble your team, activate specialists, consider the offer, reject the offer, inform your public, invoke protection, gather friends, exhaust your attacker, eliminate the attraction, and set up a new defense plan.	Tear down the stovepipes: Be sure the lines of reporting are customized for emergencies.
Adverse international events: Understand the causes, determine the gravity, move swiftly, take the long look, be patient, and return to the market.	You are stronger in the broken places: The future crisis plan is dependent on collecting knowledge of failures and successes.
Regulation and deregulation: Assess the changed climate, co-opt the power spots, exploit the inevitable, change vigorously, and settle down for tomorrow.	A lightning rod works both ways: Find good people to whom you can delegate duties.

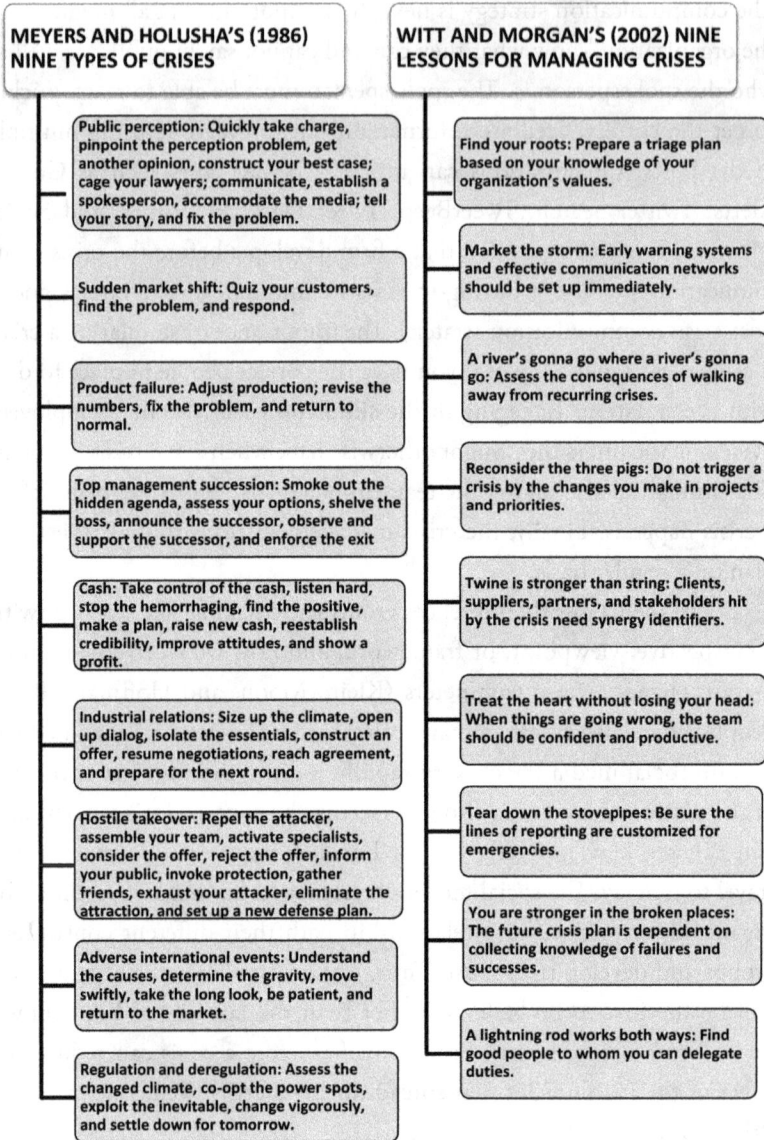

Figure 5.1 Nine types and nine lessons of managing crises

The advice from Meyers and Holushas (1986) focuses more on crises affecting larger firms, based on Meyers's extensive experience as chairman of American Motors. On the other hand, Witt and Morgan's examples are derived from experiences with both small and large companies. However, some similarities can be noted in the two bodies of thought concerning crisis management.

A company in crisis must quickly find out how much the crisis has hurt their constituents and consequently their organization. They must efficiently correct the problem and calculate how much they are willing or obligated to pay to make things right with stakeholders. If the management team or members of it are a part of the problem, the management must swiftly make changes. Advice to managers involved in a crisis response includes these steps:

- Figure out how to rectify the problem without having to go out of business.
- Try to protect your stakeholders.
- Negotiate from a position of strength as much as possible. Go for a win–win outcome but be careful about emotions getting in the way. Find people who can understand and turn the situation around.
- Always look at all options and make new plans for the future.

The Use of Argument in Crises

As a manager responding to crises, you must persuade stakeholders to agree to what the management advocates—an end to the crisis and preservation of the company's good image. When speaking to the public during a crisis, you will need to use techniques of arguing effectively, including presenting the (1) basic argument, (2) persuasion, (3) syllogism, (4) enthymeme, and (5) Toulmin's model.

To *argue* is to declare. Consequently, a basic argument can be any simple declarative sentence the speaker uses to make a claim that requires proof; for example, Jane has a cute baby; Mark will eventually get cancer because he smokes a pack of cigarettes each day; that quick rabbit will always elude that dumb hound. All the aforementioned declaratives need further proof to convince others to advocate the same sentiment. To *persuade* is to convince outside listeners to advocate that which you advocate. The Greek philosopher Aristotle devised methods for testing claims.

The *deductive syllogism* is a logical argument in which the primary and secondary premises include all the information (facts or truths) needed to form a necessary logical conclusion. If the primary and secondary premises are true, the conclusion is certain. As can be seen in Figure 5.2, in a deductive syllogism one can argue with certainty.

Deductive argument	Primary premise:	*All men will age and die.*
	Secondary premise:	*George is a man.*
	Conclusion:	*George will age and die.*

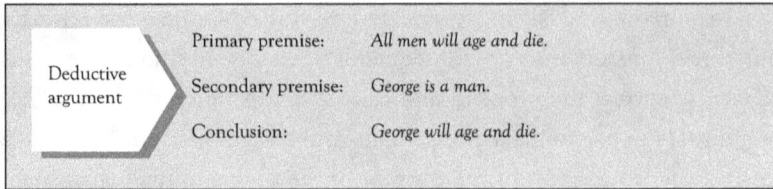

Figure 5.2 The deductive syllogism

The problem with a deductive syllogism is that, in reality, rarely do we find ideal situations in which the information we draw upon to arrive at conclusions is complete.

The *enthymeme* was Aristotle's solution to the problem he recognized with the deductive syllogism: it is not completely realistic, because people do not tend to argue that way. Deductive conclusions require perfect information on the premises, which rarely exists in real life. The enthymeme is a form of *inductive syllogism* in which the premises include "visible links," and the "missing links" are provided by the audience. The conclusion, therefore, is only a probable outcome and can never be certain one. The assumption is that audiences are reasonable, and thus worthy to supply the missing links of the argument (see Aristotle, Rhetoric, I, 1-2). In more modern terms, audiences connect the dots.

To invalidate a claim, all we need is a counter example or proof to the contrary. For example, if, in Figure 5.3, we can establish that Frank, Laura's husband, took the umbrella 5 minutes earlier than when Laura left for work, the conclusion is invalid. Therefore, the illustrated enthymeme allows one to argue inductively with merely probable conclusions. The links between the data and claim are easily broken in the enthymeme shown in Figure 5.3.

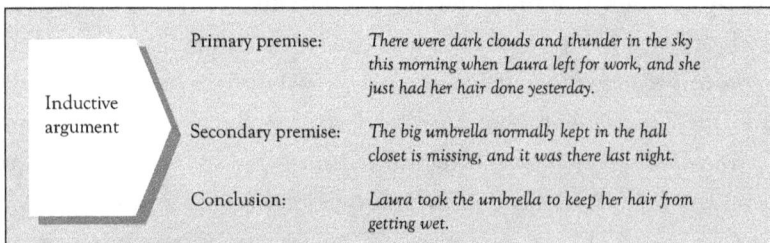

Inductive argument	Primary premise:	*There were dark clouds and thunder in the sky this morning when Laura left for work, and she just had her hair done yesterday.*
	Secondary premise:	*The big umbrella normally kept in the hall closet is missing, and it was there last night.*
	Conclusion:	*Laura took the umbrella to keep her hair from getting wet.*

Figure 5.3 The enthymeme or inductive syllogism

Toulmin (1969) found the enthymeme to be lacking in several important ways and created an extension of the argument that differs from Aristotle's enthymeme. Toulmin considers reservations or counter arguments contrary to the advocate's claims. Not all outside listeners will be in favor of the advocate's argument. In some cases, audiences will fill in the missing links to show proof to the contrary—the media or government can be counted on to provide this type of rebuttal. While Aristotle's enthymeme did not account for this consideration, Toulmin developed a way to incorporate these elements into an inductive argument.

Let us examine a declarative sentence made by the president of a hypothetical company—XYZ—which is in crisis communication mode. The company has been accused of illegally dumping a banned substance which is a toxin. The main elements of the Toulmin model are data, the facts of the argument; a qualifier, which is an estimate of the degree of certainty attributed to a claim; claims, which are conclusions to be established; warrants, which are general statements authorizing the inductive leap from data to claim; backing, which is more specific information that helps support the warrant; and reservation, which is a possible exception to a claim or warrant (Sproule 1980). The main line of proof in the Toulmin model is derived from data, warrants, and qualifiers. How Toulmin's model differs from Aristotle's enthymeme is the additional attention given to the links between the data and claim. Figure 5.4 illustrates Toulmin's extended argument.

In Figure 5.4, the invalidation of the president's conclusion is by the reservation argument. If the reservation argument is found to be true, notice how it weakens both the president's warrant (a nearly perfect Environmental Protection Agency record) and his backing (polluting risks the company's reputation). In a crisis, managers are attempting to influence outside listeners, though journalists' statements or the testimony from whistleblowers can break the links between data and claims made by the leaders of organizations under fire. Reservations will likely come from intense media and government scrutiny. During a crisis, managers should assume that the public is a group of outside listeners, who are not themselves advocates of the company's side. Therefore, crisis communication arguments require managers to prove their claims.

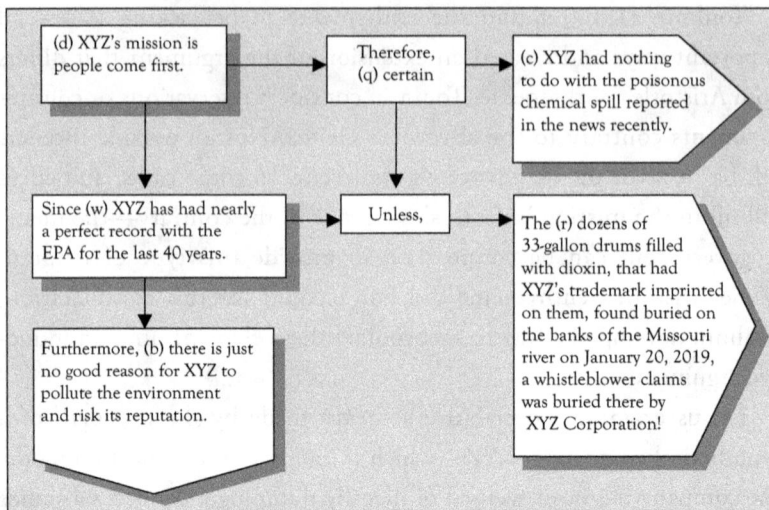

Figure 5.4 Crisis argument

Crisis Communication Mistakes

People who run large companies are intelligent people. Nevertheless, these intelligent people often make avoidable common mistakes when crises occur. These mistakes in crisis communication include (1) talking off the cuff to the media, (2) failing to identify the public's sentiment, and (3) failing to garner empathy.

Talking Off the Cuff to the Media

Often managers are not poised to be proactive but are rather reactive after being shocked into response by the tumult of a crisis. Even though history has shown that off-the-cuff speaking is often detrimental during a crisis, managers continue to make such mistakes when talking to journalists (Hoffman and Moyer 2007). Because of the replaying of management errors by intense media attention and government scrutiny, the public typically offers little sympathy and can even rebuke harshly. Eventually, managers who make mistakes in speaking off-the-cuff lose rhetorical credibility. When this happens, the crisis takes a turn for the worse. Window into Practical Reality 5.1 is an example of how the off-the-cuff remarks of a British Petroleum (BP) executive made the BP crisis worse.

Window into Practical Reality 5.1

CEO Tony Hayward's Damaging Comments to the Media

Following the BP oil spill in the Gulf of Mexico in 2011, CEO Tony Hayward's comments to the media escalated emotions, drew harsh media response, and intensified government scrutiny. The result was the further disruption in BP's daily business operations, a tarnished personal and company image, and a serious plunge in BP's stock prices. Hayward's slip-of-the-lip, off-the-cuff conversation caused enormous negative publicity for BP. When he uttered the words "There's no one who wants this thing over more than I do, you know, I'd like my life back," during the worst oil-related off-shore environmental disaster in American history, a domino effect was triggered leading to his ouster as BP's CEO. The company's response was not surprising. According to a 2006 Corporation Reputation Watch by the PR firm Hill & Knowlton, 85 percent of analysts surveyed said that a CEO should leave the company after engaging in behavior that has a negative impact on the company's reputation (Valentine 2007).

CEO Hayward failed to acknowledge the severity of loss and the fact that the American public had been bombarded by the media coverage of the tragedy and devastation of the oil spill. While 11 people had lost their lives, enormous damage had been done to the ecosystem and to the livelihoods of thousands, his selfish utterance signaled to the public that Hayward clearly did not understand the depth of pain BP had caused the people in the Gulf region.

Failing to grasp the magnitude of the public's sentiment is a pitfall for many executives reacting to a crisis-turned mega-tsunami. Following Hayward's callous statement, he was demonized by the American public.

When managers recognize that a negative turning point has occurred, it is time for them to undertake targeted internal and external communication, before a debacle can occur. When managers make mistakes in talking to journalists before a strategy is in place, they inadvertently increase the risk that a prodromal crisis will occur, with even more devastating consequences.

Failing to Identify the Public's Sentiment

The public's receptivity to managerial arguments hinges on how the management responds in an attempt to influence sentiment, while at the same time resolving the crisis. As a manager, it is important that you understand how to structure the messages to manage crises from both the internal as well as external perspectives. When an organization is in crisis mode, it is easy for managers to forget that internal communications can be as important as external communications. Managerial crisis communication fails most often when managers misconstrue the public's true sentiment surrounding a crisis. Managers fail to favorably influence outside listeners—the public—when they do not understand the use of argument in crisis situations. Window into Practical Reality 5.2 shares an example of football star Michael Vick's interview with the media which ended in disaster for the athlete.

Window into Practical Reality 5.2

Underestimating the Passion People Have for Their Pets

On April 2007, 51 pitbulls were seized from football player Michael Vick's compound, and the star was charged with operating an illegal dog fighting operation. Although Michael Vick had been picked first in the NFL draft in 2001, his athletic stardom did little to diminish the outcry from the public, once they learned of the extent of the cruelty shown to the animals. Vick made public denials to the press and appeared to lack understanding of the seriousness of his personal crisis. Vick was under the faulty impression that his celebrity status might save him from public outcry for justice for the dogs. Although Michael Vick served some jail time over the crime, he signed a lucrative 6-year contract with the Philadelphia Eagles in 2011 worth $100 million and returned to the NFL (Gorant 2008).

- Do you suppose that Mr. Vick is now wiser and sensitive to public response?
- How important was Vick's management team in gauging public sentiment?

The media largely drives what people think, even when supporting facts are lacking. Public officials from the local to the federal levels were held in disdain by the American public due to their actions in the aftermath of Hurricane Katrina. Illustrating this phenomenon are the media reports of New Orleans Mayor C. Ray Nagin stating that someone had allegedly fired on a rescue helicopter; while not proven, the report stopped rescue attempts for many hours (Garnett and Kouzmin 2007). The media also chose not to report that the mayor and state governor would not allow federal troops to provide assistance.

President George W. Bush also received his share of the public's ire in regard to his handling of relief efforts following Katrina. When President Bush prematurely praised the then Federal Emergency Management Agency (FEMA) director Michael Brown by saying, "Brownie, you're doing a heck-of-a-job," the casual sounding statement started a domino effect of negative response. The public's view was that he appeared disconnected from the magnitude of the Hurricane Katrina disaster. President Bush's declaration that Michael Brown was "doing a heck-of-a-job" failed to resonate well with outside listeners, who saw so much of continuing human suffering.

President Bush describes in his memoirs that one of the worst days in his presidency was when he heard hip-hop star Kanye West tell journalists, during the height of the Katrina disaster, that "George Bush doesn't care about Black people." Although West never directly called Bush a racist, Bush and many others interpreted West's argument to mean just that.

In commenting on the Hurricane Katrina disaster, Cole and Fellows (2008) noted that when certain types of communications fail and a crisis has become chronic, the situation evolves into a mega-tsunami. They drew several conclusions for responding effectively to a crisis that (1) effective care communication is of little value if the subsequent actions and crisis messages are inadequate; (2) message preparation before the crisis is essential; (3) messages must be credible to their recipient audiences; and (4) adaptation for ethnicity, class, gender, and similar demographic characteristics must occur, if risk communication messages are to be effective. They concluded that during the Hurricane Katrina disaster, message clarity was frequently lacking, and those speaking with journalists often lacked sufficient credibility. Post Katrina interviews by company spokespersons and government officials illustrate a classic failure to properly adapt to critical audiences, resulting in overall ineffective crisis communication.

A good example of responding appropriately to the public's sentiment occurred when the Obama-appointed Secretary of the United States Department of Agriculture (USDA), Tom Vilsack, had to eat crow over the Shirley Sherrod issue. Public officials had accused Sherrod of being racist, and Vilsack terminated her employment with the USDA without legal due process. It was learned that the charge was based on misinformation stemming from a 2-minute excerpt of a speech that Sherrod had delivered nearly 20 years earlier. Vilsack publicly apologized immediately to Sherrod and offered her job back. His actions were possibly driven by his own moral fortitude, but certainly by his sensitivity to the public's sentiment. The public outcry was calmed when Vilsack (1) admitted fault, (2) acknowledged the truth, and (3) publicly apologized. President Obama also made it public knowledge that he had called Sherrod and apologized.

The prodromal crisis surge in the Sherrod case never did evolve into a mega-tsunami because of strategic actions taken by Vilsack and Obama. Argenti and Forman (2002) argue that a crisis has the elements of high drama and catharsis, crafted by journalists and readers alike. If Sherrod had been resolute in her anger toward the two government officials, who assumed responsibility for her wrongful termination, it is possible the public's ire would have turned on her for being unreasonable.

Failing to Unify Empathy

The best way to avoid being insensitive during a crisis is to refocus managerial thinking into collective empathy. *Empathy* is having a direct emotional connection to the feelings and experiences of others' suffering. Every single manager in the organization should read and understand the crisis plan, and general agreement should be reached among them about the internal perspective of the public's sentiment (Wester 2009). Executives must make an attempt to genuinely feel a personal consequence for the problems their firm is associated with causing. Being empathetic means investigating and relating to hurt, with a deeper understanding of those who are hurting, regardless of culpability. It is likely that BP CEO Hayward never would have uttered those infamous words had he and his team of managers focused on a singular message of empathy for the families of the 11 people who died on the drilling platform.

Nevertheless, CEOs seeking to communicate empathy must be careful when they apologize to the public, because an apology perceived by the public to be disingenuous can backfire and worsen the crisis situation. Window into Practical Reality 5.3 provides an example of how a Wells Fargo CEO was forced to resign because his public apology seemed insincere.

Window into Practical Reality 5.3

Stumpf's Resignation from Wells Fargo Prompted by His Insincere Apology

Years after Wells Fargo began firing employees en masse for creating fake accounts in order to meet aggressive cross-selling goals, one of Wells Fargo's highest ranking executives said he didn't think there was a problem with the bank's sales culture. (Gandel 2016, para 1)

Of course, for Wells Fargo CEO John Stumpf, the level of public outcry from his remarks meant only one thing. Caving to public pressure, Stumpf was forced to resign from Wells Fargo, costing him an estimated $41 million in compensation and benefits.

Wells Fargo was fined $185 million in penalties in a settlement for its creation of phony accounts. The company had created phony accounts in the names of unsuspecting bank customers. The bank reported that 5,300 employees involved in the fraud were fired from their positions.

In September 2016, a month earlier, while being grilled by lawmakers on Capitol Hill, Stumpf said he was "deeply sorry" but denied that the bank had engaged in an orchestrated effort to defraud customers. According to Cox (2016, para 11) "Despite Stumpf's apologies, critics have been frustrated over his denials that the behavior went beyond rogue employees and reflected a systematic approach by the bank." Senators and the public perceived Stumpf's apology to be insincere and lacking empathy (Cox 2016).

The potential number of unauthorized accounts is estimated to be 3.5 million according to a recent internal audit. The public scandal was largely due to a corporate culture that incentivized the behavior, suppressed discovery of the wrongdoing, and "toppled Wells Fargo's previous chief executive, John G. Stumpf." The fraud ignited public outcry. Customers, lawmakers, and regulators were incensed by the bank's denials. The United States Justice Department and a few state attorneys generals continue to investigate Wells Fargo (Cowley 2017). When the public perceives a CEO to be dishonest, pretending to have empathy for others' suffering, they will put extreme collective pressure on the company that in most cases will force the CEO to resign from the organization in crisis.

- If a company is clearly in the wrong, is it a good idea for the CEO to apologize to the public?
- Was there any way that CEO Stumpf could have appeased the public, the U.S. Senate?
- Is there any way any CEO of Wells Fargo could have used communication skills to convey genuine empathy and survive the public's scrutiny during this type of crisis?
- How is the Wells Fargo apology different than the Shirley Sherrod apology that was successfully delivered by the Obama Administration?

The formulation of an effective internal communication strategy is essential to the survival of an organization following a crisis. Figure 5.5 shows four-step process that management should consider when developing an internal communication strategy.

Each of the steps in the process require careful consideration. Figure 5.6 shows four communication techniques needed while implementing a crisis strategy (Gasser 1989).

Because of the interdisciplinary nature of internal communications, an integrated approach to internal communication is beneficial in order to maintain crucial knowledge sharing between the organization units. An integrated perspective draws from the domains of business, management,

Fourth,

weigh the risks and benefits involved.

Third,

determine the method of communication.

Second,

determine and analyze the intended audience.

First,

clearly identify the purpose of communication.

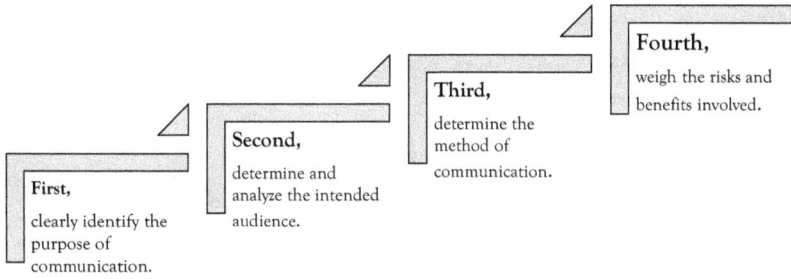

Figure 5.5 Four-step process for an internal communication strategy

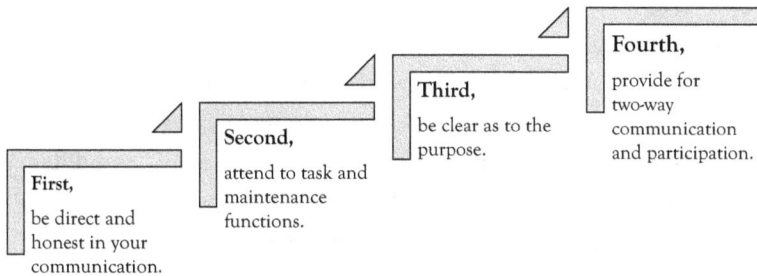

Fourth,

provide for two-way communication and participation.

Third,

be clear as to the purpose.

Second,

attend to task and maintenance functions.

First,

be direct and honest in your communication.

Figure 5.6 Four communication techniques while implementing crisis strategy

corporate, and organizational communications. Both practical and theoretical knowledge are essential, as well as understanding the types of formal and informal communications taking place within the organization (Kalla 2005).

CEOs should not count on organizational spokespersons to single-handedly quash negative publicity. When Caliero, Taylor, and Ungureanu (2009) examined the image repair tactics of 17 fraud-related and mismanaged crises, they found that news releases posted on organizations' websites were effective in responding to media news reports of the crises, thus giving organizations an opportunity to tell their sides of the stories.

Risk communication can be seen as a sister process to crisis communication, and achieving the goals for both processes depends on having a well-written risk and crisis communication plan (Ferrante 2010). Additionally, businesses that have engaged in socially responsible rhetoric appear better able to use this social responsibility history to their advantage. Companies with an established reputation for corporate so-cial responsibility (CSR) have a better chance of integrating the crisis communication message aspects of their CSR message, and the public better receives this integration than companies that do not have an established record of CSR. Moreover, the length of a company's in-volvement in CSR matters when it uses CSR claims during crisis com-munication to counter negative publicity. It also appears that religion, cultural similarity, and sensitivity impact the repair and rebuilding of the public's perception in crisis management (Heath, Lee, and Ni 2009; Legg 2009).

A crisis management plan should address how the organization will control the situation and quickly gather information. It should also ad-dress the setup of a centralized crisis management center that will allow the company to communicate early and often to the media and different constituents, all while keeping the business operating. The plan should also address how to include local first-response teams.

Steps for maintaining continual backup of all IT and communica-tions systems in an offsite location must be part of the comprehensive crisis management plan. When the Twin Towers went down, as well as during Hurricane Katrina, what saved many of the affected companies were their offsite backup systems. Using the web to get accurate infor-mation to the public as soon as possible is also a good idea. Some of the worst things a company can do during a crisis are pretending noth-ing is going on, letting your reputation take care of the situation, and treating the media as the enemy. Other errors in response include using language that the stakeholders do not understand and addressing only the issues and not the feelings. While prompt response is desirable, an organization should avoid guessing at the damages and wait for fac-tual information. Probably the two most deadly errors an organization can make in a crisis are continuing to do the same thing when it is not working, and being reactive rather than proactive in their response (Bernstein 2004).

As presented in Window into Practical Reality 5.4, the *Gettysburg Ad-dress* can be viewed as a 2-minute crisis management speech that served two purposes: honoring fallen heroes, and appealing to the citizenry that they should continue support for fighting the Civil War.

Window into Practical Reality 5.4

President Abraham Lincoln's Gettysburg Address in Pennsylvania, November 19, 1863

(a) *Four score and 7 years ago our fathers brought forth on this continent,* a new nation; (b) *conceived in liberty,* and dedicated to the proposition that all men are created equal. (c) *Now we are engaged in a great civil war,* testing whether that nation or any nation so conceived and so dedicated, can long endure. We are met on a great battlefield of that war. We have come to dedicate a portion of that field, as a final resting place for those who here gave their lives that that nation might live. It is altogether fitting and proper that we should do this.

But in a larger sense, (d) *we cannot dedicate—we cannot consecrate—we cannot hallow*—this ground.

The brave men, living and dead, who struggled here, have consecrated it, far above our poor power to add or detract. The world will little note, nor long remember, what we say here, but it can never forget what they did here. It is for us the living, rather, to be dedicated here to the unfinished work which they who fought here have thus far so nobly advanced. It is rather for us to be here dedicated to the great task remaining before us—that from these honored dead we take increased devotion to that cause for which they gave the last full measure of devotion—that we here highly resolve that these dead shall not have died in vain—(e) *that this nation, under God, shall have a new birth of freedom—and that government of the people, by the people, for the people, shall not perish from the earth.*

Lincoln used (a) allusion, (b) litotes, (c) tautology, (d) metaphor, and (e) impassioned hyperbole to forcefully make his memorable points. *Allusion* is defined as a reference to an historical event. A *metaphor* compares by referring to one thing as another. A *litotes* states the obvious as if denying its opposite or makes a deliberate understatement of the factual happenings. *Tautology* is the repetitious use of a word or phrase in close succession, and an *impassioned hyperbole* is a rhetorical exaggeration used to heighten emotional meaning. Can you think of other speeches in which these techniques were used to influence the audience positively?

President Abraham Lincoln's *Gettysburg Address* can be described as his recovery speech for the American Civil War. With the creative use of figures of speech (words that heighten rhetorical effect), Lincoln honored in Gettysburg, Pennsylvania, the 45,000 dead while at the same time attempted to persuade the North to continue with a war that many did not endorse. Lincoln used language devices to spark such visual clarity in the minds of his hearers that it became impossible for them to deny the truth value of his declarative sentences. One declarative sentence is sufficient to be an argument, and a collection of simple sentences is sufficient to constitute an extended argument. In other words, a great speech is persuasive because it appears to be a collection of undeniable declarative sentences that influences many people, even beyond its immediate end.

Lincoln was able to influence outside listeners through argument. It is apparent that Lincoln also understood the nature of proof by example and the importance of figures of speech in argument. Lincoln's deliberate use of pictorial language is an example of the type of mental images executives should be attempting to impose on the minds of their hearers during a crisis in order to sway influence to the point of view they advocate. The best way to avoid drab, unemotional language is to plan for the use of stylistic touches when talking to internal constituents as well as journalists.

As unpopular as the Civil War was for Lincoln, with a nation on the brink of collapse, Lincoln was able to use an oratory opportunity to salvage commitment. When he uttered the declarative sentences ". . . dedicated here to the unfinished work . . . resolve that these dead shall not have died in vain" these sentences collectively represent what is now an immortal extended argument.

Summary

Crisis, from a business-oriented point of view, is a negative turning point. Crisis begins with a prodromal situation that runs the risk of (1) escalating emotions, (2) drawing harsh media or government scrutiny, (3) disrupting daily business operations, (4) tarnishing the business's image or the image of its executives, or (5) causing profits to plummet. Crisis management planning is paramount in avoiding an escalation of a prodromal crisis situation to one where the CEO is pressured to resign from public outcries and stakeholder pressure.

The BP oil spill disaster evolved into a much larger crisis because of the various mistakes in communication which gave the impression to the public that BP was uncaring and unresponsive. When President Bush used casual language to praise FEMA director Michael Brown's response to Hurricane Katrina while not acknowledging the horrors that people were facing, the public's view was that he was disconnected with the magnitude of the disaster.

Managers who make mistakes when speaking to the media run the risk of losing their rhetorical credibility. This fact strikes at the heart of the importance of proper communication techniques in crises situations. Managers who address the public during such crises must not only be armed with facts but also be sure they have correctly identified with the feelings of the people involved and that they adequately project empathy. Managers speaking to the public must be sincere in their apologies and should apologize without denial of the facts. Insincere apologies coupled with denial can backfire and worsen the crisis situation.

USDA secretary Vilsack and President Obama were able to avoid the escalation of a prodromal situation to a full-blown crisis by (1) admitting fault, (2) acknowledging the truth, and (3) publicly apologizing.

Abraham Lincoln used various language devices to spark visual clarity in the minds of the listeners and inspire their acceptance of his declarative sentences. Managers engaged in crisis communication can learn valuable lessons from those who have successfully maneuvered through difficult situations by using carefully planned responses and masterfully crafted public messages.

CHAPTER 6

Communication Audits

Objectives

After reading this chapter, you will be able to:

1. describe the purpose and process of a communication audit;
2. determine appropriate communication audit goals and activities;
3. explain how to conduct reliable and valid communication audits;
4. write an effective communication audit report;
5. explain the strategic implications of communication audit results for goal achievement;
6. identify potential pitfalls of communication audits.

Introduction

Organizations routinely evaluate the effectiveness of programs and employees; however, they rarely evaluate the communication that takes place within the firm. Such audits are seldom done, even though communication networks are the mechanism through which employees receive information on how to do their jobs. Without good communication practices, firms will face challenges in getting their products to the market, making a profit, or retaining their employees. Communication affects the organizational structure and management success of a firm.

A *communication audit* is "a comprehensive and thorough study of communication philosophy, concepts, structure, flow, and practice within an organization" (Emmanuel 1985, p. 50). A communication audit typically includes an assessment of the quality of the communication within an organization, as well as its goals and activities. The audit can be thought of as a type of test. Different types of communication audits are recognized by the International Communication Association (ICA). Managers conduct communication audits to discover how information flows, how information gets blocked, and how people perceive and react to the information that they receive. The questions asked during a communication audit are critical, as they determine the information that we receive. When conducting an audit, caution should be exercised to make sure that the information sought does not mask the communication problems that exist.

In this chapter, we will discuss the necessary steps in conducting proper communication audits, which include (1) defining the communication audit; (2) conducting a reliable and valid communication audit; (3) selecting the appropriate communication audit goals and activities; (4) writing a report of the communication audit results; (5) analyzing the strategic implication of audit results on the achievement of the goal; and (6) anticipating the pitfalls of communication audits.

Selecting Audit Methods

The communication audit is a way of gathering data to analyze the communication that takes place within the firm. It provides the management with insight as to what is actually happening, rather than what they think is happening, during communications. The value of communication audits to organizations have been verified in numerous studies. A communication audit should include five processes (Gordon 2001):

- Develop a picture of the communication in the organization including major topics, sources, and channels of communication.
- Look at specific communication tools and describe their value and relevance.
- Determine how the employees are receiving messages: downward, upward, horizontally, and externally—and whether those experiences are positive or negative.
- Provide information to develop a strategic plan for improving the quality of communication.
- Provide a process to continually measure communication effectiveness in the organization.

Obviously, the audit process should reflect the needs of the particular firm. Instruments should be worded to fit the terminology used in the organization, and questions should be included that reflect the position of particular internal groups, including that of international and virtual members.

A company must gather useful information that will help improve internal communications. Once the parameters of the audit have been determined, it is possible to select the correct audit activities and determine who should conduct the communication audit. Should internal or external people do the audit? Though internal entities know the organization best, employees may share information more truthfully with outsiders. Data gathering options must be considered for collecting the most accurate information—questionnaire, interviews, communication logs, and such. Employees will need the assurance that all information collected will be confidential, and sometimes this is easier done with external auditors. Careful interpretations and presentation of the findings by the researchers is essential so that managers can weigh the results properly. Management should be engaged in the process and willing to make changes that are indicated in the audit. If management is not willing to act on the data, then there is no reason to collect it.

Reliable and Valid Measures

Communication audits must measure accurately the multidimensional aspects of the constructs under study. A *construct* is an attribute of a person that often cannot be measured directly, but which can be assessed using a number of indicators or variables. Constructs will have one or more dimensions or component parts. For example, if you are conducting a communication audit and wish to measure the managerial listening skills practiced within an organization, measuring whether managers engage in good or bad listening behaviors would be a hidden, or latent, variable with two dimensions. A manager's ability to listen well would naturally be the hidden variable of the listening construct. You cannot directly observe whether the listening taking place in the head of the manager is good or bad; therefore, the best way to understand good and bad managerial listening practices is for you to develop a reliable and valid questionnaire.

A *reliable* measure is one that is trustworthy and consistent, and does not show inconsistent degrees or magnitudes with each application—an inch is always an inch regardless of what is being measured. A measure that is *valid* measures what it is purported (designed) to measure. It would not be valid to measure social drinking, for example, with a questionnaire that you designed specifically to measure recreational drug use. Therefore, communication audits must measure multidimensional constructs accurately. Figure 6.1 illustrates the essential goals and the information-gathering activities used in a successful communication audit to assess the quality of communication.

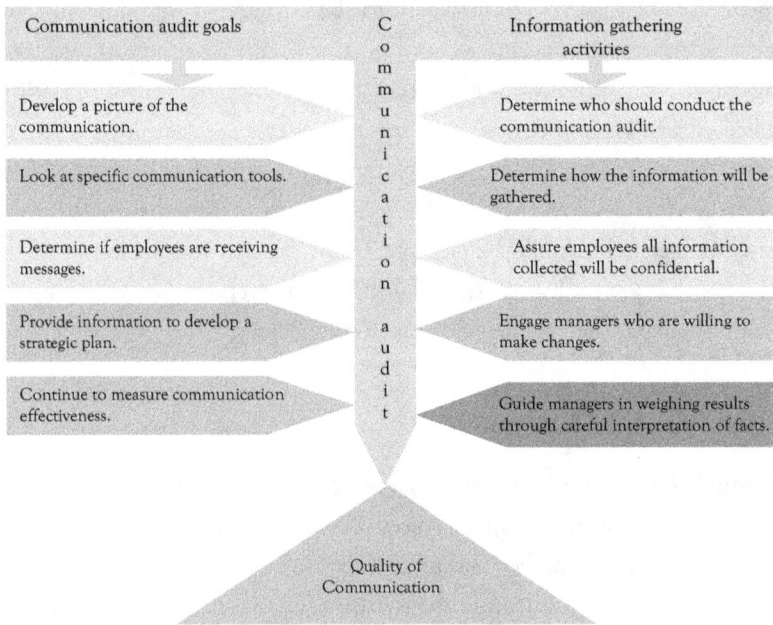

Communication audit goals	Communication audit	Information gathering activities
Develop a picture of the communication.		Determine who should conduct the communication audit.
Look at specific communication tools.		Determine how the information will be gathered.
Determine if employees are receiving messages.		Assure employees all information collected will be confidential.
Provide information to develop a strategic plan.		Engage managers who are willing to make changes.
Continue to measure communication effectiveness.		Guide managers in weighing results through careful interpretation of facts.

Quality of Communication

Figure 6.1 Essential communication audit goals and information-gathering activities

Communication Audit Approaches

The approach used in the communication audit should be selected based upon the outcomes the audit will provide, the process the audit will take, and the perspectives of the multiple stakeholders. Managers may want to improve an aspect of communication or develop an intervention to sort out a problem. They may want to examine and analyze the communication processes that are occurring, or they may want to identify the views of employees concerning the communication (Hogard and Ellis 2006). After determining the communication facets that should be studied, the management will need to select the instruments to be used, choose an appropriate research method, collect, and analyze the data. A number of approaches exist for conducting communication audits, which include the use of focus groups, communication logs, direct observation, interviews, surveys, content analysis, skills testing, and blended approaches that use a combination of these methods.

Focus groups consist of members of the organization who are brought together to discuss the organization's communication issues. The data collector may be the group facilitator or another individual designated for that purpose. The researchers compile and compare the information to draw conclusions. In cases where there are large quantities of information involved or many personnel, *communication logs* may be necessary to capture and catalog the communication activities. All participating individuals are to be instructed to keep a log, or diary, in which they record meetings, telephone conversations, texts, e-mails, face-to-face meetings, and any documents that are read. At the conclusion of the designated logging period, the researchers will examine and code the diaries and analyze the frequency of various types of communication.

Direct observation involves following a subject around and recording information about the person's communications. Then a researcher codes and statistically analyzes the participant's communication activities. Observation is generally more reliable than communication logs because someone else is watching and recording rather than the individual self-reporting. It is easy for someone keeping a diary to forget to write things down, and some may even feel that the activity is a waste of time and not take the task seriously.

During *interviews*, a researcher meets with individuals and discusses communication issues using a set of prepared questions. It is important to use the same set of questions for all interviewees so that a comparison of responses is possible. A particular type of interview is the *critical incident interview,* in which employees are asked about a given real or hypothetical communication incident.

Surveys conducted through questionnaires are easy for researchers to analyze and can be the easiest and least expensive method of gathering data from a large group of people. Another positive of this method is the anonymity that it offers the survey respondent. The wording of questions is very important, and allowing participants to provide written comments can provide additional information for consideration in the audit.

Content analysis involves the careful examination of documents produced by the employees of a firm. Content analysis can be performed on a wide array of communications including e-mail messages, letters, memos, recorded meetings, employee newsletters, policies, job advertisements, posted in-house signs, contracts and forms, invoices, and orientation and training materials. Content analysis can be coupled with interviews or surveys to yield even more information.

Skill testing involves designing a means for evaluating the communication skill levels of workers. Once the skill level of employees is determined, goals can be established for increasing worker effectiveness.

The *blended approach* is a combination of two or more of the aforementioned audit approaches. Most communication audits involve multiple methods to gain as much information as possible. Who should perform the analysis is also a question that the management must consider. Will people respond better to outsiders or insiders? Figure 6.2 summarizes seven essential elements in a thorough communication audit (Dodd 2008).

Communication Audit Instruments

The ICA's questionnaire audit has been widely used for the study of organizational communication. The comprehensive instrument has 13 sections and includes five measurement tools: surveys, interviews, network analyses, communication experiences, and communication diaries. The completion of the instrument is dependent on the recollection and reporting of critical communication incidents by the responder. The nine topic areas of the ICA questionnaire are shown in Figure 6.3.

The Communication Satisfaction Questionnaire (CSQ) is another survey to measure the relationship between communication and productivity. Figure 6.3 also illustrates the eight dimensions of the CSQ that have been found to be reliable and valid (Crino and White 1981; Hecht 1978). The questionnaire links communication satisfaction and productivity

Dodd's seven audit items	1. Leadership and administrative style—X, Y, or Z leadership style: Are people or tasks more important, and what contingencies are used? (e.g., X are autocratic managers, Y are managers who will listen, and Z uses an inclusive management style)
	2. Structural elements—flat or tall organization chart, bureaucratic or team-oriented management, span of control, and information flow
	3. Interpersonal communication and relationships—trust, expectations, feedback, information disclosure, listening, and feeling part of a team
	4. Nonverbal issues—image, informational signage, lighting, colors, smells, status conveyed, open versus closed body language, and employee dress and image
	5. Employee issues—communication satisfaction, safety, benefits, and complaints
	6. Customer issues—product quality, delivery and timing, and service
	7. Competition—new products and services, customer preferences, and retaining of customers

Figure 6.2 Seven Essential Elements in an Audit

across eight dimensions. Clampitt and Downs (1993) tested the CSQ in two organizations and found that communication was perceived to have an above-average impact on productivity and that communication satisfaction factors differentially impacted productivity. Personal *feedback* had a significant impact on productivity in both companies. (Recall the discussion of feedback in Chapter 2 of *Managerial Communication for Organizational Development.*) While it was interesting that communication with coworkers, meetings, memos, and corporate-wide information had relatively low impacts on productivity, the supervisors' information was critical. Employees in higher level positions, as compared to non-supervisory employees, said that receiving information about the corporation significantly impacted their productivity. One recent study found that when the gender variable was controlled, it had no influence on the feedback employees were willing to give. However, "Training influenced an individual's proclivity to give feedback to others, even when gender was held constant" (Roebuck, Bell, and Hanscom 2016, p. 6). Managers implementing communication audits should be aware that feedback training influences the willingness of employees to provide feedback.

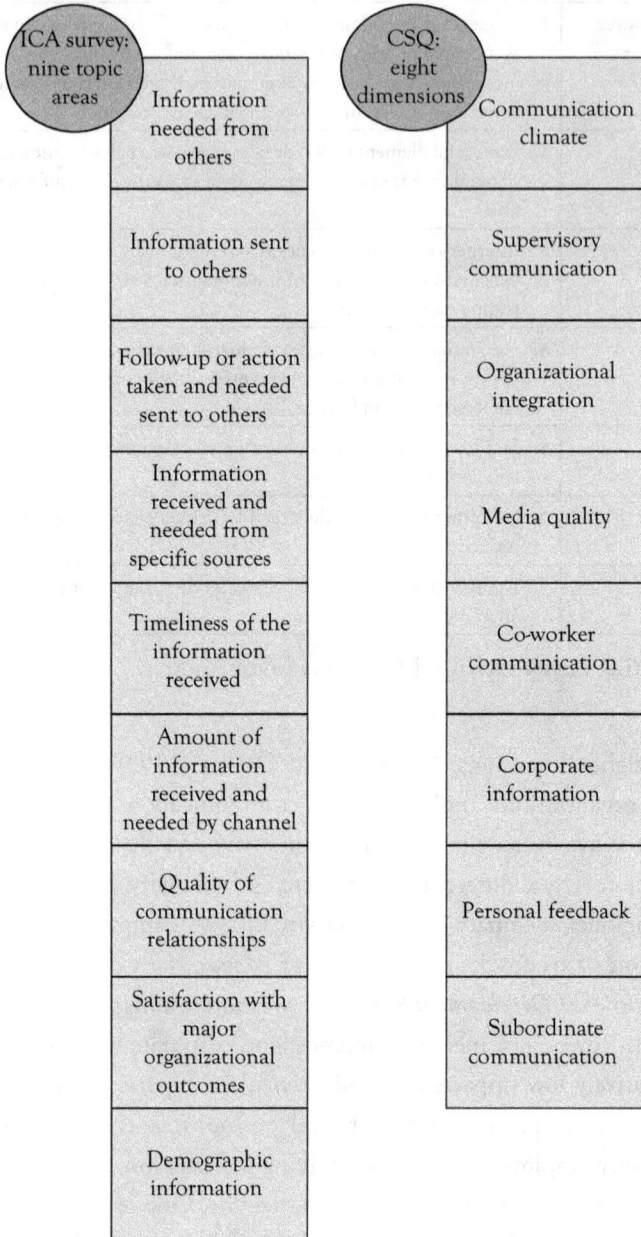

ICA survey: nine topic areas	CSQ: eight dimensions
Information needed from others	Communication climate
Information sent to others	Supervisory communication
Follow-up or action taken and needed sent to others	Organizational integration
Information received and needed from specific sources	Media quality
Timeliness of the information received	Co-worker communication
Amount of information received and needed by channel	Corporate information
Quality of communication relationships	Personal feedback
Satisfaction with major organizational outcomes	Subordinate communication
Demographic information	

Figure 6.3 Comparison of two communication audit instruments:
ICA and CSQ

Optimizing the Communication Audit

The climate within an organization impacts information flow within the firm. A communication audit will help determine if the culture of the organization is supportive or defensive about news and ideas. If managers are indifferent, manipulative, or superior in their attitudes toward subordinates, the subordinates will stop trying to communicate. If managers promise items and do not carry through on their promises, their credibility will quickly erode. Employees generally want openness and transparency in information and are much more likely to share information if they feel supported. If employees are included in decisions and not just told what to do, they feel much more a part of the organization. Figure 6.4 illustrates Daly's (1992) seven tests of communication skills needed for optimal audits.

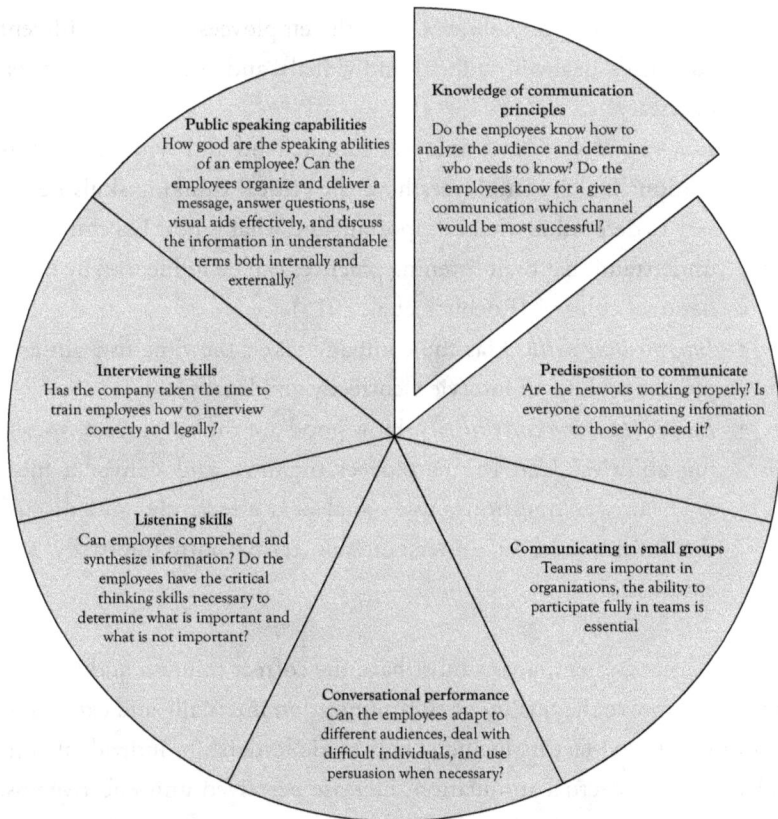

Knowledge of communication principles
Do the employees know how to analyze the audience and determine who needs to know? Do the employees know for a given communication which channel would be most successful?

Public speaking capabilities
How good are the speaking abilities of an employee? Can the employees organize and deliver a message, answer questions, use visual aids effectively, and discuss the information in understandable terms both internally and externally?

Interviewing skills
Has the company taken the time to train employees how to interview correctly and legally?

Predisposition to communicate
Are the networks working properly? Is everyone communicating information to those who need it?

Listening skills
Can employees comprehend and synthesize information? Do the employees have the critical thinking skills necessary to determine what is important and what is not important?

Communicating in small groups
Teams are important in organizations, the ability to participate fully in teams is essential

Conversational performance
Can the employees adapt to different audiences, deal with difficult individuals, and use persuasion when necessary?

Figure 6.4 Daly's (1992) seven tests for communication skills needed for optimal audits

Each of the seven tests involves answering key questions about communication within the organization:

- *Knowledge of communication* principles is predicated on answering key questions.
- *Predisposition to communicate* refers to whether the networks function properly. Is everyone communicating information to those who need it? Do the employees know how to analyze the audience and determine who needs to know? Do the employees know which channel would be most successful for a given communication?
- *Communicating in small groups.* How important are teams to organization? How capable are employees of participating as fully on teams as necessary?
- *Conversational performance.* Can the employees adapt to different audiences, deal with difficult individuals, and use persuasion when necessary?
- *Listening skills.* Can employees comprehend and synthesize information? Do the employees have the critical thinking skills necessary to determine what is important and what is not? Do employees understand that their listening practices can be influenced by international culture? (Roebuck et al. 2015)
- *Interviewing skills.* Has the company taken the time to train employees on how to interview correctly and legally?
- *Public speaking capabilities.* How good are the employees' speaking abilities? Can the employees organize and deliver a message, answer questions, use visual aids effectively, and discuss the information in understandable terms both internally and externally?

Managers and employees must have the correct mindset and skills in order to improve the quality of communication internally and externally. Transformational factors include charismatic leadership, individual consideration, intellectual stimulation, increase perceived unit effectiveness, and subordinate satisfaction.

Communication Audit Report Writing

As with any test, the validity and reliability of a communication audit instrument is important. For the results to be useful, you must report the results to the people who can use the information to make changes. It is helpful to give users recommendations and a suggested implementation schedule, along with the findings. Obviously, positive information is easier to convey than negative information, which may be met with defensiveness. No one in the organization wants to be told that they are the problem. A communication audit is only valuable if the individuals within the firm are willing to accept criticism, and the organization culture affirms embracing the criticism and making the changes necessary to improve.

In sharing the results of a communication audit, it is important to have meetings with employees at the various levels within the organization. Results must be reported in a way that everyone understands what the communication audit has revealed about the organization and its relationships.

Group discussions should then be reaffirmed in other ways, such as through newsletters or individual meetings with personnel. Employee buy-in is imperative if changes are to be made. Recommendations may be structural in nature, such as changing reporting structures, or centralizing or decentralizing communication functions. Recommendations may include adjusting the priorities of the firm to give more resources and attention to particular areas of the operation. Suggestions for changing reporting requirements also may come out of the audit. Many times such actions are recommended to end turf wars that cause barriers within the firm. Recommendations may also suggest new processes or solutions to the problems. It is important to actually implement the recommended, and not just recognize the problems.

Strategic Implications of Audit Results

The results of communication audits allow managers to develop communication strategies discussed in earlier chapters. Communication strategies directly relate to the communication climate of a firm, the management orientation of firm, and whether it is bureaucratic or team oriented.

Management orientation refers to whether the leader is a macromanager or a micromanager. The more micromanagement oriented a leader is, the less say others have in the communication that happens in the firm. The more macro-oriented the leader is, the more others are free to communicate in the firm. Changing strategies and goals is not easy as people tend to resist change. If you are successful in changing the climate, it will be because you have effectively anticipated employees' reactions to the changes, and you have communicated honestly and openly with them.

Some executives' personalities make it easier for them to successfully implement strategy changes because they naturally inspire the employees to follow them. However, all executives can educate their employees through training, helping employees to develop their own goals and linking them to corporate goals, distinguishing fact from rumor, and developing a positive climate. If a climate of common purpose is developed, and all employees understand their part in that purpose, then they feel a rapport and relationship with other employees and management. Addressing the effectiveness of the total spectrum of communication—upwards, downwards, horizontally, internally, and externally—is imperative to changing the communication climate of an organization. Change, however, is not always achieved without a price, as shown in Window into Practical Reality 6.1.

Window into Practical Reality 6.1

The Fallout of Change

A few years ago, an organization decided it wanted to empower its employees and become more team-oriented rather than bureaucratic in its management approach. While some employees embraced the concept, others did not believe that the managers would truly change. Others did not want to take on the responsibility of making decisions, just wanting to come in and do their jobs and leave. Trust was a major issue between some employees and management. In following the changes over a period of time, both the management and workers who stayed with the firm liked the team environment. However, the company lost some managers and workers who could not make the transition. Sometimes an organizational change is so much of an upheaval to individuals that they must leave and find a position elsewhere.

What makes a communication change strategy successful? First, the people who have to implement the changes must give legitimacy to the goals and process. Workers must have a way of being able to articulate what is working and not working, concerning the new communication strategies, in an environment of mutual trust. Employees must see how it affects them personally. Many times this means working through the confusion and ambiguity of a new communication structure.

Figure 6.5 illustrates a strategic model developed by Robertson (2005) to measure managerial communication climate. The model includes five major elements: information openness, open and supportive communication climate, interactive supportiveness, five managerial information sharing practice, and eleven managerial interaction skills.

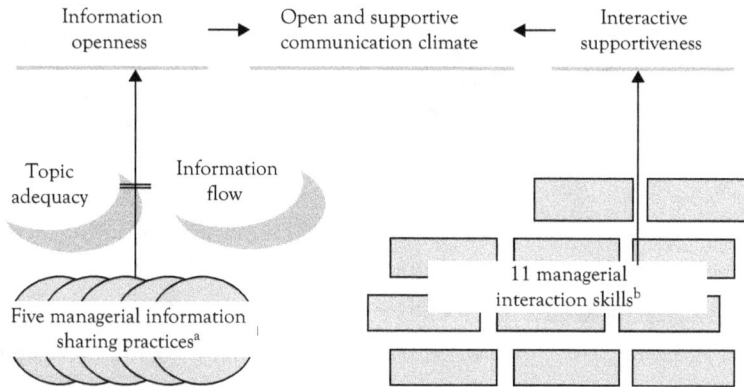

Figure 6.5 Robertson's managerial communication climate model

[a]Job information, personal information, operational information, strategic information, and upward information.
[b]Active listening, empathic listening, checking accuracy, clarifying meaning, disclosing emotions, encouraging input, providing feedback, soliciting feedback, giving instructions, managing conflict, and constructive feedback.

Information openness refers to the mechanical process that happens as information moves from sender to receiver and back. Topic adequacy addresses the ability of information to flow when needed. Information flow is the free exchange of ideas, issues, and opinions. The five information sharing practices include communicating job information, personal information, operational information, strategic information, and upward information. Interaction supportiveness refers to how people communicate and whether their interactions are affirming or disaffirming. The 11 managerial interaction skills include active listening, empathic listening, checking accuracy, clarifying meaning, disclosing emotions, encouraging input, providing feedback, soliciting feedback, giving instructions, managing conflict, and providing constructive feedback. The Robertson model illustrates how managerial communication competence can create open and supportive communication, understanding, meaning, and good relationships.

Implementation of change strategies is important, and managers often discover that repetition can help people retain the message. Another strategy is to identify and utilize opinion leaders, as they are influential in getting others to follow. Managers must be careful in identifying actual problems and describing them accurately. Mislabeling issues can lead to attempting to solve the wrong problems (Minter 2010). A little emotional intelligence and common sense can go a long way in implementing new communication strategies!

Pitfalls of Communication Audits

While audits can be used to improve communication and thus increase morale and productivity, they do not always produce positive results. If the management uses the results of an audit to punish employees, the overall health of the organization will suffer. If there are hidden agendas, employees will know soon enough, and many may leave the organization, or worse, sabotage projects. Avoid common pitfalls by clearly notifying everybody of the objectives, goals, and scope of the audit before it is conducted and assuring them that the overall intent is to improve the communication within the firm.

Summary

Over time, most firms will have problems with communication because of changes in personnel, poor training, growth, structural changes, or other internal factors. A communication audit is an assessment of the quality of communication within the organization. The audit assists in determining what and where the problems exist. While there are many communication audit tools available, a firm first needs to know its own needs in order to select or customize the communication audit that will work best for them. It is generally best to use outside consultants to gather, analyze, and suggest corrections to the communications of the organization, as employees may feel freer to share their perceptions, and anonymity is better protected. Finding where the bottlenecks are in the communication networks and reducing them can be very beneficial to an organization. The communication climate and the willingness of individuals to work toward improving their communication skills are essential to progress. Without a mindset of improvement by employees at all levels, the organization will have difficulty in implementing communication change.

When conducting a communication audit, the facets of communication to be tested must be determined, an appropriate instrument selected and modified if necessary, appropriate research methods used, the information collection carefully completed, and an analysis of the data accurately performed. Formulating and implementing a strategy is possible once these steps are completed. Developing a strategic plan for improvement that fits the situation and that is supported by employees at all levels is essential to the process of change. Everyone who is impacted by the audit should be informed of the objectives, goals, and scope of the audit before it is conducted, and assured that the overall intent is to improve the communication within the firm.

References

Chapter 1

Bates, S. 2007. "The Eight Most Frequent Mistakes People Make in Front of an Audience." *Business Strategy Series* 8, no. 4, pp. 311–17.

Bell, R.L. 2011. "Is Your Speech Filled With Um? Three Tips to Eliminate Filled Pauses from Your Professional Presentation." *Supervision* 72, no. 10, pp. 10–13.

Bender, P.U. 1991. "Secrets of Power Presentations." *The Canadian Manager* 16, no. 3, pp. 16–19.

"Creating Pictographs." 2010. http://rheck.com, (accessed March 15, 2014).

Detz, J. 2007. "12 Tips to Improve Your Next Presentation: Learning How to Communicate." *Vital Speeches of the Day* 73, no. 12, pp. 540–42.

Detz, J. 2014. *How to Write & Give A Speech*. 3rd ed. New York, NY: St. Martin's Press, pp. 147–65.

Gardner, H.E. 1993. *Multiple Intelligences: The Theory in Practice, a Reader*. New York, NY: Basic Books, pp. 25–37.

Goleman, D. 1995. *Emotional Intelligence: Why It Can Matter More Than IQ*. New York, NY: Bantam Books.

Howell, P., and S. Sackin. 2001. "Function Word Repetitions Emerge When Speakers Are Operantly Conditioned to Reduce Frequency of Silent Pauses." *Journal of Psycholinguistic Research* 30, no. 5, pp. 457–74.

McKenzie, S. 2002. "Break Nervous Habits Before They Become Distractions." *Presentations* 16, no. 2, p. 62.

Parrish, W.M., and R. Murphy. 1947. *Speaking in Public*. New York, NY: Charles Scribner's Sons.

Patton, G. May 17, 1944. "Pep Talk to Troops on D-Day." www.speeches-usa.com/Transcripts/george_patton-dday.html, (accessed March 15, 2014).

Rankin, K. January 5, 2018. "2017 Police Shootings by the Numbers," *Colorlines: Art & Culture*. https://www.colorlines.com/articles/2017-police-shooting-numbers, (accessed May 23, 2018).

Roosevelt, F.D. December 8, 1941. "Declaration of War." www.speeches-usa.com/Transcripts/franklin_roosevelt-december7th.html, (accessed March 15, 2014).

Sandford, W., and W. Yeager. 1942. *Principles of Effective Speaking*. 4th ed. New York, NY: The Ronald Press Company.

Schachter, S., N. Christenfeld, B. Ravina, and F. Bilous. 1991. "Speech Disfluency and the Structure of Knowledge." *Journal of Personality and Social Psychology* 60, no. 3, pp. 362–67.

Stanton, N., 2009. *Mastering Communication*. 5th ed. New York, NY: Palgrave Macmillan.

Turner, L.H., and K. Dindia. 1995. "An Investigation of Female/Male Verbal Behaviors in Same-Sex and Mixed-Sex Conversations." *Communication Reports* 8, no. 2, pp. 83–99.

Chapter 2

Buss, D.M. 1987. "Selection, Evocation, and Manipulation." *Journal of Personality and Social Psychology* 53, pp. 1214–21.

Claveria, K. March 23, 2015. "Cause Marketing Gone Wrong: What Sparked the Starbucks 'Race Together' Backlash," *VISIONCRITICAL*. https://www.visioncritical.com/race-together-pr-fiasco/, (accessed May 25, 2018).

Crane, E., and F.G. Crane. 2002. "Usage and Effectiveness of Impression Management Strategies in Organizational Settings." *Journal of Group Psychotherapy, Psychodrama, & Sociometry* 55, no. 1, pp. 25–34.

Gardner, W.L. 1992. "Lessons in Organization Dramaturgy: The Art of Impression Management." *Organizational Dynamics* 21, pp. 33–47.

Gardner, W.L., and M.L. Martinko. 1988. "Impression Management in Organizations." *Journal of Management* 14, pp. 321–38.

Goffman, E. 1959. *The Presentation of Self in Everyday Life*. New York, NY: The Overlook Press.

Gordon, R.A. 1996. "Impact of Ingratiation on Judgments and Evaluations: A Meta-Analytic Investigation." *Journal of Social Psychology* 71,
pp. 54–70.

James, M.S.L., and Shaw, J.C. 2016 "Cynicism Across Levels in the
Organization." *Journal of Managerial Issues* 28, no. 1–2, p. 83.

Jones, E.E., and T.S. Pittman. 1982. "Toward a General Theory of
Strategic Self Presentation." In *Psychological Perspectives on the Self,* ed.
J. Suls. Hillsdale, NJ: Erlbaum, pp. 231–62.

Kacmar, K.M., and D.S. Carlson. 1999. "Effectiveness of Impression
Management Tactics Across Human Resource Situations." *Journal of
Applied Social Psychology* 29, pp. 1293–315.

Kramer, N.C., M. Feurstein, J.P. Kluck, Y. Meier, M. Rother, and
S. Winter. February 16, 2017. "Beware of Selfies: The Impact of
Photo Type on Impression Formation Based on Social Networking
Profiles." *Frontiers in Psychology* 8, pp. 2–14.

Larkin, M. March 24, 2017. "Not-so-free speech! Jersey Shore star Snooki's
$32K Rutgers fee paves way for passage of bill limiting speaking payments at
public colleges." *Daily Mail Online.* https://news.rutgers.edu/sites/medrel/
files/news-clips/Not-so-free%20speech%21%20Jersey%20Shore%20
star%20Snooki%27s%20%2432k%20Rutgers%20fee%20paves%20
way%20for%20passage%20of%20bill%20limiting%20speaking%
20payments%20at%20public%20colleges.pdf. (accessed January 7, 2019).

Nelson, D.L., and J.C. Quick. 2003. *Organizational Behavior.* Mason,
OH: South-Western.

Potter, P.W. 2014. "The Role of Ingratiation in Heightening Suspi-
cion." *Journal of Organizational Culture, Communications and
Conflict* 18, no. 1, pp. 129–137.

Reiman, T. 2008. "First Impressions Really Matter." *Communication
World* 25, no. 4, pp. 29–31.

Ridoutt, B.G., R.D. Ball, and S.K. Killerby. 2002. "Wood in the Interior Office Environment: Effects on Interpersonal Perception." *Forest
Products Journal* 52, no. 9, pp. 23–30.

Riggio, R.E., and H.S. Friedman. 1986. "Impression Formation: The
Role of Expressive Behavior." *Journal of Personality and Social Psychology* 50, no. 2, pp. 421–27.

Rogers, A. April 3, 2012. "15 of the Most Ridiculous Celebrity Splurges of All Time." *Business Insider.* https://www.businessinsider.com/ridiculous-celebrity-purchases-2012-4 (accessed January 7, 2019).

Scheibe, K.P., J.C. McElroy, and E.C. Morrow. 2009. "Object Language and Impression Management." *Communications of the ACM* 52, no. 4, pp. 129–31.

Seiter, J.S. 2007. "Ingratiation and Gratuity: The Effect of Complimenting Customers on Tipping Behavior in Restaurants." *Journal of Applied Social Psychology* 37, no. 3, pp. 478–85.

Snyder, M., and W. Ickles. 1985. "Personality and Social Behavior." In *Handbook of Social Psychology*, eds. G. Lindzey, and E. Aronson. Vol. 2. New York, NY: Random House, pp. 883–947.

Swann,W.B., Jr. 1987. "Identity Negotiation: Where Two Roads Meet." *Journal of Personality and Social Psychology* 53, pp. 1038–51.

Chapter 3

Adams, J.S. 1963. "Toward an Understanding of Inequity." *Journal of Abnormal and Social Psychology* 67, no. 5, pp. 422–36.

Balloch, J. January, 2010."Defamation Lawsuit Dismissal Upheld: Appeals Court Affirms Judge's Decision on Case," *McClatchy-Tribune Business News.* http://www.mctdirect.com/preview.php?id=201001161027MCT_____ REG_NEWS12363_32262, (accessed January 16, 2010).

Bell, R.L., and J.S. Martin. April, 2010. "Techniques for Writing a Reprimand: How to Modify the Behavior of a Rule Breaker at Work." *Supervision* 71, no. 4, pp. 8–12.

Bell, R.L., and J.S. Martin. 2012. "The Relevance of Scientific Management and Equity Theory in Everyday Managerial Communication Situations." *Journal of Management Policy and Practice* 13, no. 3, pp. 106–15.

Bell, R.L., and R. Ramdass. 2010. "A Model for Reprimanding Unproductive Workplace Behaviors." *Supervision* 71, no. 3, pp. 3–6.

Bynum, T. November 10, 2017. "The Degree Doesn't Make You a Rock Star, but These Typos will." MSP on LinkedIn.

Drucker, P.F. 1974. *Management: Tasks, Responsibilities, and Practices.* New York, NY: Harper and Row.

Drucker, P.F. 1954. *The Practice of Management.* 1st ed. New York, NY: Harper and Row, Publishers.

EEOC. January 25, 2018. "EEOC Releases Fiscal Year 2017 Enforcement and Litigation Data." https://www.eeoc.gov/eeoc/newsroom/release/1-25-18.cfm

EEOC. November 17, 2017. "EEOC Regulations." www.eeoc.gov/laws/regulations

Gabor, A. 2000. *The Capitalist Philosophers: The Geniuses of Modern Business—Their Lives, Times and Ideas.* New York, NY: Times Books.

Peck. J.A., and J. Lewashina. February 15, 2017. "Impression Management and Interview and Job Performance Ratings: A Meta-analysis of Research Design with Tactics in Mind." *Frontier in Psychology* 8, no. 201, pp. 1–10.

Pfeil, M.P, A.B. Setterberg, and J.S. O'Rourke IV. 2003. "The Art of Downsizing: Communicating Lay-Offs to Key Stakeholders." *Journal of Communication Management* 8, no. 2, pp. 130–41.

Taylor, F.W. 1998. *The Principles of Scientific Management.* Mineloa, NY: Dover Publications.

Thomas, L. January 12, 2018. "Walmart's Bonuses: Here's What Workers Will Receive." *CNBC.* https://www.cnbc.com/2018/01/12/walmarts-bonuses-heres-what-workers-will-receive.html, (accessed May 29, 2018).

Thomas, L., and C. Reagan. January 11, 2018. "Walmart to Raise Its Starting Wage to $11, Give Some Employees Bonuses Following the Bill Passage," *CNBC.* https://www.cnbc.com/2018/01/11/walmart-to-boost-starting-wage-give-employees-bonus-after-tax-bill.html, (accessed May 27, 2018).

Vroom, V.H. 1964. *Work and Motivation.* New York, NY: John Wiley and Sons.

Walmart. May 20, 2011. "Supreme Court Decision in Wal-Mart Class-Action Claim Brings Praise, Anger," *Fox News.* http://www.foxnews.com/politics/2011/06/20/groups-blast-laud-high-court-for-decision-against-nations-largest/#, (accessed December 11, 2013).

Chapter 4

Barnett, C.K., and N. Tichy. 2000. "How New Leaders Learn to Take Charge." *Organizational Dynamics* 29, no. 1, pp. 16–32.

Barrett, D.J. 2002. "Change Communication: Using Strategic Employee Communication to Facilitate Major Change." *Corporate Communications,* 7, no. 4, pp. 219–31.

Bennis, W.G., and B. Nanus. 1985. *Leaders: Strategies for Taking Charge.* New York, NY: Harper & Row.

Burlew, L.D., J.E. Pederson, and B. Bradley. 1994. "The Reaction of Managers to the Pre-Acquisition Stage of a Corporate Merger: A Qualitative Study." *Journal of Career Development* 21, no. 1, pp. 11–22.

Conger, J.A. 1991. "Inspiring Others: The Language of Leadership." *The Executive* 5, no. 1, pp. 31–45.

Dewhurst, S., and L. Fitzpatrick. 2007. "Bringing Out the Excellent Communicator in Managers." *Strategic Communication Management* 11, no. 5, pp. 20–23.

Douglas, C., J.S. Martin, and R.H. Krapels. 2006. "Communication in the Transition to Self-Directed Work Teams." *Journal of Business Communication* 43, no. 4, pp. 295–321.

Drucker, P.F. 1974. *Management: Tasks, Responsibilities, and Practices.* New York, NY: Harper & Row.

Duck, J.D. 2001. *The Change Monster: the Human forces that Fuel or Foil Corporate Transformation & Change.* New York, NY: Crown Business.

Edwards, B.A. 2000. "Chief Executive Officer Behavior: The Catalyst for Strategic Alignment." *International Journal of Value-Based Management* 13, no. 1, pp. 47–54.

Elgin, S.H. 1980. *The Gentle Art of Verbal Self-Defense.* New York, NY: Dorset Press.

Frahm, J., and K. Brown. 2007. "First Steps: Linking Change Communication to Change Receptivity." *Journal of Organizational Change Management* 20, no. 3, pp. 370–87.

Jones, L., B. Watson, E. Hobman, P. Bordia, C. Gallois, and V.J. Callan. 2008. "Employee Perceptions of Organizational Change: Impact of Hierarchical Level." *Leadership & Organization Development Journal* 29, no. 4, pp. 294–316.

Lipman, V. February 8, 2016. "Why Does Organizational Change Usually Fail? New Study Provides Simple Answer," *Forbes*. https://www.forbes.com/sites/victorlipman/2016/02/08/why-does-organizational-change-usually-fail-new-study-provides-simple-answer/#24cbe8374bf8, (accessed June 9, 2018).

McCay, K., J.R.C. Kuntz, and K. Naswell. 2013. "The Effect of Affective Commitment, Communication, and Participation on Resistance to Change: The Role of Change Readiness." *New Zealand Journal of Psychology* 42, no. 2, pp. 29–40.

O'Neill, M. March 1, 2011. "How Netflix Bankrupted and Destroyed Blockbuster," *Business Insider*. http://www.businessinsider.com/how-netflix-bankrupted-and-destroyed-blockbuster-infographic-2011-3, (accessed June 4, 2018).

Ross, B., and J. Rhee. 2008. "Big Three CEOS Flew Private Jets to Plead for Public Funds," *ABC News,* http://abcnews.go.com/Blotter/Wall-Street/story?id=6285739&page=2, (accessed November 25, 2009).

Shaw, A. 2013. "This Is the End' for Blockbuster Video." https://abcnews.go.com/Business/blockbusters-rental-end/story?id=20863987

Smeltzer, L.R. 1991. "An Analysis of Strategies for Announcing Organization-Wide Change." *Group and Organization Studies* 16, no. 1, pp. 5–24.

Smeltzer, L.R., and M.F. Zener. 1992. "Development of a Model for Announcing Major Layoffs." *Group and Organization Studies* 17, no. 4, pp. 446–72.

Spears, M.C., and D. Parker. 2002. "Framing Decisions to Communicate Change." *Journal of Organizational Culture, Communication, and Conflict* 6, no. 2, pp. 65–72.

Suchan, J. 2006. "Changing Organizational Communication Practices and Norms." *Journal of Business and Technical Communication* 20, no. 1, pp. 5–47.

Tharp, P. December 29, 2000. "Montgomery Ward's Last Chapter; Catalog Pioneer Folding, to Fire 37,000, Shut 250 Stores," *New York Post*. https://nypost.com/2000/12/29/montgomery-wards-last-chapter-catalog-pioneer-folding-to-fire-37000-shut-250-stores/, (accessed June 4, 2018).

Wiggins, L. 2008. "Managing the Ups and Downs of Change Communication." *SCM* 13, no. 1, pp. 20–23.

Wolper, J. May, 2016. "Making Change Management Successful." *Talent Development (TD)*, p. 16.

Chapter 5

Argenti, P.A., and J. Forman. 2002. *The Power of Corporate Communication: Crafting the Voice and Image of Your Business.* New York, NY: McGraw-Hill, p. 235.

Bernstein, J. 2004. "Making a Crisis Worse: The Biggest Mistakes in Crisis Communication." https://www.bernsteincrisismanagement.com/newsletter/crisismgr011001.html (accessed January 7, 2019).

Caldiero, C., M. Taylor, and L. Ungureanu. 2009. "Image Repair Tactics and Information Subsidies During Fraud Crises." *Journal of Public Relations Research* 21, no. 2, pp. 218–28.

Cole, T.W., and K. Fellows. 2008. "Risk Communication Failure: A Case Study of New Orleans And Hurricane Katrina." *The Southern Communication Journal* 73, no. 3, pp. 211–28.

Coombs, W.T. 2007. "Protecting Organization Reputations During a Crisis: The Development and Application of Situational Crisis Communication Theory." *Corporate Reputation Review* 10, no. 3, pp. 163–76.

Cowley, S. 2017. "Wells Fargo Review Finds 1.4 million More Suspect Accounts," *The New York Times.* https://www.nytimes.com/2017/08/31/business/dealbook/wells-fargo-accounts.html, (accessed July 25, 2018).

Cox, J. 2016. "Wells CEO John Stumpf Says He Is 'Deeply Sorry' but Denies 'Orchestrated Effort'," *CNBC.* https://www.cnbc.com/2016/09/29/wells-ceo-john-stumpf-says-he-is-deeply-sorry-but-denies-orchestrated-effort.html, (accessed July 25, 2018).

Ferrante, P. 2010. "Risk and Crisis Communication." *Professional Safety* 55, no. 6, pp. 38–45.

Fink, S. 1986. *Crisis Management: Planning for the Inevitable.* New York, NY: AMACOM.

Gandel, S. October 13, 2016. "New Wells Fargo CEO Just Months Ago Denied the Bank Had a Sales Problem," *FORTUNE.* http://fortune.com/2016/10/13/wells-fargo-scandal-tim-sloan-ceo/, (accessed July 25, 2018).

Garnett, J.L., and A. Kouzmin. 2007. "Communicating Throughout Katrina: Competing and Complementary Conceptual Lenses on Crisis Communication." *Public Administration Review* 67, pp. 171–88

Gasser, L. 1989. "Designing Internal Communication Strategies: A Critical Org." *Employment Relations Today* 16, no. 4, pp. 273–82.

Gorant, J. 2008. "What Happened to Michael Vick's dogs …." https://www.si.com/more-sports/2008/12/23/vick-dogs, (accessed January 7, 2019).

Heath, R.L., Lee, J., and L. Ni. 2009. "Crisis and Risk Approaches To Emergency Management Planning and Communication: The Role of Similarity and Sensitivity." *Journal of Public Relations Research* 21, no. 2, pp. 123–41.

Hoffman, J., and J. Moyer. 2007. "Are You Ready For the TV Cameras? Communicating with the Media and the Public Following Negative Incidents." *American Water Works Association Journal* 99, no. 5, pp. 48–49.

Kalla, H.K. 2005. "Integrated Internal Communications: A Multidisciplinary Perspective." *Corporate Communications* 10, no. 4, pp. 302–14.

Kessel, M., and R. Masella. 2016. "Preparing for Crises." *Nature Biotechnology* 34, no. 2, pp. 133–36.

Klein, G., Moon, B., and Hoffman, R.R. 2006. "Making sense of sensemaking 1: Alternative perspectives." *IEEE intelligent systems* 21, no. 4, pp. 70–73. https://www.computer.org/csdl/mags/ex/2006/04/x4070-abs.html

Legg, K.L. 2009. "Religious Celebrity: An Analysis of Image Repair Discourse." *Journal of Public Relations Research* 21, no. 2, pp. 240–50.

Meyers, G.C., and J. Holusha. 1986. *When It Hits the Fan: Managing the Nine Crises of Business.* Boston, MA: Houghton Mifflin Company.

Sproule, M.J. 1980. *Argument: Language and Its Influence.* New York, NY: McGraw-Hill Boole Company.

Toulmin, S.E. 1969. *The Uses of Argument.* Cambridge, MA: University Press.

Valentine, L. 2007. "Talk is Not Cheap." *ABA Banking Journal* 99, no. 12, pp. 38–41.

Veil, S.R., T. Buehner, and M.J. Palenchar. 2011. "A Work in Process Literature Review: Incorporating Social Media in Risk and Crisis

Communication," *Journal of Contingencies and Crisis Management* 19, no. 2, pp. 110–22.

Wester, M. 2009. "Cause and Consequences of Crises: How Perception Can Influence Communication." *Journal of Contingencies and Crisis Management* 17, no. 2, pp. 118–25.

Witt, J.L., and J. Morgan. 2002. *Stronger In the Broken Places: Nine Lessons for Turning Crisis into Triumph.* New York, NY: Time Books—Henry Holt and Company.

Chapter 6

Clamplitt, P.G., and C.W. Downs. 1993. "Employee Perceptions of the Relationship Between Communication and Productivity: A Field Study." *The Journal of Business Communication* 30, no. 1, pp. 5–30.

Crino, M.D., and M.C. White. 1981. "Satisfaction in Communication: An Examination of the Downs-Hazen Measure." *Psychological Reports* 49, pp. 831–38.

Daly, J. November, 1992. "Assessing Speaking and Listening: Preliminary Considerations for a National Assessment." *National Assessment of College Students Learning: Identification of Skills to be Taught, Learned, and Assessed.* A Report on the Proceedings of the Second Study Design Workshop, U.S. Department of Education. NCES94–286.

Dodd, C.H. 2008. *Managing Business and Professional Communication.* 2nd ed. Boston, MA: Pearson.

Emmanuel, M. 1985. "Auditing Communication Practices." In *Inside Organizational Communication,* eds. C. Reuss, and R. Desilvas. New York, NY: Longman.

Gordon, G. 2001. "A Buyer's Guide to Communication Audits." *Journal of Employee Communication Management* 51.

Hecht, M.L. 1978. "Measures of Communication Satisfaction." *Human Communication Research* 4, pp. 350–68.

Hogard, E., and R. Ellis. 2006. "Evaluation and Communication: Using a Communication Audit to Evaluate Organizational Communication." *Evaluation Review* 30, no. 2, pp. 171–87.

Minter, R. 2010. "Organizational Communication Audits: Assessing Core Communication Competencies Within the Organization."

International Journal of Management and Information Systems 14, no. 5, pp. 107–18.

Robertson, E. 2005. "Placing Leaders at the Heart of Organizational Communication." *SCM* 9, no. 5, pp. 34–37.

Roebuck, D.B., R.L. Bell, R. Raina, and C.E. Lee. 2015. "Comparing Perceived Listening Behavior Differences Between Managers and Nonmanagers Living in the United States, India, and Malaysia," *International Journal of Business Communication* 53, no. 4, pp. 485–518.

Roebuck, D.B., R.L. Bell, and M.E. Hanscom. 2016. "Differences in the Observed Frequency Distributions of Male and Female Feedback Behaviors." *Journal of Applied Management and Entrepreneurship* 21, no. 2, pp. 6–25.

About the Authors

Reginald L. Bell is a professor of management in the College of Business at Prairie View A&M University. He received his PhD in business education from the University of Missouri at Columbia. He has several dozen articles published in peer-reviewed journals and proceedings and is a frequent contributor to *Supervision*. Bell serves as an ad hoc reviewer for the *International Journal of Business Communication* and the *Journal of Business and Technical Communication*; he serves on the editorial review board for the *Business and Professional Communication Quarterly*. His research has also appeared in the *Business and Professional Communication Quarterly, International Journal of Business Communication, Interdisciplinary Journal of E-Learning and Learning Objects, Journal of Applied Management and Entrepreneurship, Journal of Education for Business*, and *the Journal of Management Policy and Practice*.

Jeanette S. Martin is a professor emeritus in the School of Business at the University of Mississippi. She received her EdD in business education from the University of Memphis. She was previously a reviewer and associate editor for the *Journal of Business Communication* and reviewer for the *International Association of Intercultural Relations*. Her research has appeared in the *Journal of Education for Business, Journal of Business Communication, Management Communication Quarterly*, and others. She has published three books: *Global Business Etiquette, The Essential Guide to Business Etiquette, Passport to Success, a chapter in Handbook of Ethnic Conflict,* and a textbook *Intercultural Business Communication*.

Index

OTHER TITLES IN OUR CORPORATE COMMUNICATION COLLECTION

Debbie DuFrene, Stephen F. Austin State University, *Editor*

- *How to Write Brilliant Business Blogs, Volume I: The Skills and Techniques You Need* by Suzan St. Maur
- *How to Write Brilliant Business Blogs, Volume II: What to Write About* by Suzan St. Maur
- *Public Speaking Kaleidoscope* by Rakesh Godhwani
- *The Presentation Book for Senior Managers: An Essential Step by Step Guide to Structuring and Delivering Effective Speeches* by Jay Surti
- *Managerial Communication and the Brain: Applying Neuroscience to Leadership Practices* by Dirk Remley
- *Communicating to Lead and Motivate* by William C. Sharbrough
- *64 Surefire Strategies for Being Understood When Communicating with Co-Workers* by Walter St. John
- *Business Research Reporting* by Dorinda Clippinger
- *English Business Jargon and Slang: How to Use It and What It Really Means* by Suzan St. Maur
- *Conducting Business Across Borders: Effective Communication in English with Non-Native Speakers* by Adrian Wallwork
- *Strategic Thinking and Writing* by Michael Edmondson
- *Business Report Guides: Research Reports and Business Plans* by Dorinda Clippinger
- *Business Report Guides: Routine and Nonroutine Reports and Policies, Procedures, and Instructions* by Dorinda Clippinger
- *Managerial Communication For Organizational Development* by Reginald L. Bell and Jeanette S. Martin

Announcing the Business Expert Press Digital Library

Concise e-books business students need for classroom and research

This book can also be purchased in an e-book collection by your library as

- *a one-time purchase,*
- *that is owned forever,*
- *allows for simultaneous readers,*
- *has no restrictions on printing, and*
- *can be downloaded as PDFs from within the library community.*

Our digital library collections are a great solution to beat the rising cost of textbooks. E-books can be loaded into their course management systems or onto students' e-book readers. The **Business Expert Press** digital libraries are very affordable, with no obligation to buy in future years. For more information, please visit **www.businessexpertpress.com/librarians**. To set up a trial in the United States, please email **sales@businessexpertpress.com**.

www.ingramcontent.com/pod-product-compliance
Lightning Source LLC
Chambersburg PA
CBHW061323220326
41599CB00026B/5000